CHURCH WORSHIP
AND THE
NON-CHURCHGOER

CHURCH WORSHIP
AND THE
NON-CHURCHGOER

A Handbook for Clergy and Teachers

BY

GORDON W. IRESON

DIOCESAN MISSIONER OF EXETER
AND HON. CHAPLAIN TO THE BISHOP OF EXETER

LONDON

NATIONAL SOCIETY
69, GREAT PETER STREET
WESTMINSTER, S.W.1

SOCIETY FOR PROMOTING
CHRISTIAN KNOWLEDGE
NORTHUMBERLAND AVENUE, W.C.2

THIS BOOK IS PRODUCED IN COM-
PLETE CONFORMITY WITH THE
AUTHORISED ECONOMY STANDARDS

First printed 1944

MADE IN GREAT BRITAIN

PREFACE

THIS little book was originally intended to be something quite different from what it is. I was asked to read a paper at the first meeting of the Church of England Youth Council's Commission on *Youth and Christian Worship*, officially set up to investigate the most effective ways of introducing young people to Christian Worship, and so training them that they become regular Communicants, and men and women of daily prayer. Subsequently I was asked by this Commission to body the substance of the paper, together with further practical illustrations, in a pamphlet designed for youth leaders.

But when I set out upon this task, I found it impossible either to allocate to youth a special category in the sphere of worship, or to think at all clearly of the subject except in relation to the whole field of evangelism and liturgy. Hence, inevitably, I found myself thinking not in terms of youth and youth leaders, but of clergy and the problem of the non-churchgoer. The pamphlet for which I had been asked just 'wouldn't come'. This little book came instead. The members of the Commission were, however, kind enough to appreciate my difficulty and to allow me thus to depart from my original terms of reference.

To some it may seem as if the case I have tried to make has been overstated; that my attitude is intransigent, if not reactionary. I can only say that it is the outcome of experience. Ten years ago I belonged to the 'gallant and high-hearted happiness' school. I believed that public worship to be 'relevant' should have a strong element of 'human interest', even if this meant considerable modification of the God-ward emphasis of the Prayer Book. Indeed, I did not hesitate to do a little re-editing of Mattins and Evensong in the light of these convictions. But I found the results extremely disappointing. The newspapers and the local cinema could provide much more 'human interest' than I could. Gradually I came to realise the folly of trying to make the Christian Faith (and the liturgy which proclaimed it) fit modern people, instead of trying to fit modern people for the Christian Faith, and I began to change the emphasis and direction of my work accordingly.

Although in the following pages I have based the case for loyalty to the Prayer Book on religious and theological grounds, I should like to make it clear that I do not regard these as the sole considerations. We are facing a situation in which any idea that the Church of England possesses a *corpus* of faith and worship has almost entirely disappeared among the laity. For this lamentable state of affairs local departures from the Prayer Book services have been largely responsible. When a parish priest makes changes in the public services, from however worthy motives, he is unconsciously undermining the authority of the Church, and suggesting to the members of his congregation that he (and not the Church) is their authority in matters of faith and worship. He need not be surprised, therefore, when some of them tell him that they prefer Mr So-and-So's teaching to his own. The only way out of our present chaos is loyal adherence to the Prayer Book rite in public services.

The principles and methods described in the following chapters have been hammered out during the last seven years in the actual conduct of teaching and worship-training groups (a high proportion of which have been youth groups) in a great variety of places. I hope that they may be of sufficient practical value to cover deficiencies of writing due partly to lack of adequate time, and partly (I fear) to lack of writing ability.

The writing owes much to the encouragement of three friends, the Rev. R. J. Hooper, the Rev. F. S. P. Girdlestone and the Rev. H. de Candole, all of whom have read parts of the book in typescript and made many useful suggestions. I am grateful to the Rev. H. P. Thompson for permission to quote from his book, *Worship in Other Lands*, and to the Rev. J. P. P. Gorton, vicar of Goldington, for allowing me to reproduce in Appendix A the service drawn up by him for the S.P.G. Festival at St. Paul's, Bedford. My thanks are also due to the Rev. F. E. Le Grice of St. Michael's, Paignton, for the account of his lantern-slide experiment, and to the Rev. P. J. Lamb, Vicar of St. Aidan's, Leeds, for his letter, both of which are reproduced in Chapter VI. Nor can I omit to thank my fellow-members of the Worship Commission for their patience with one who, when asked for an egg, produced a scorpion, and especially the Secretary, the Rev. R. D. Say, for expediting the said scorpion's passage through the press.

Finally, let me place on record that I owe much to many of my brother clergy of the Exeter diocese with whom in small groups and cells I have discussed these matters, and who have allowed me to experiment in their parishes. To them, in particular, I offer this little book with affection and respect.

GORDON W. IRESON.

Exeter,
 April 1944

" I will pray with the spirit, and I will pray with the understanding also; I will sing with the spirit, and I will sing with the understanding also."—I Cor. xiv. 15.

CONTENTS

EVANGELISM TODAY

1. *The Recovery of the Gospel.*

FOR a Christian these are stirring days. The war which is breaking up modern man-centred civilisation is also calling the bluff of the philosophy of self-sufficient humanism with its theological counterpart, modernist liberalism, and is driving us back to the fundamentals of our Faith. When journalists describe this situation, as they are apt to do, as a ' challenge to religion ', they reveal a singularly superficial understanding of the real condition of society. It is as if a patient who has consistently disobeyed his doctor's explicit instructions, and now finds himself at the point of death, should regard himself as a ' challenge to medicine '. It is not the Christian Faith that is being called in question, but the whole basis of modern civilisation.

Yet this does not give Christians the right to say in superior fashion to a broken world, ' I told you so '. Penitence and humility were never more clearly incumbent on those who profess the Christian Faith. For we have allowed the Eternal Gospel of Redemption to become watered down to an ethical idealism commonly described as Christianity, content merely to reflect the current philosophy of liberal optimism and to cover it with a thin veneer of Christian sentimentality.[1]

In one sense this process of dilution was natural, if not inevitable. The work of Darwin and his followers put the keystone into the arch of a humanist philosophy the founda-

---

[1] This is, of course, a generalisation, to which there are notable exceptions. Anglo-Catholics and definite Evangelicals have both held fast to the Gospel of Redemption, but these apart, this tendency has been true of the Church as a whole.

tions of which were laid in the Renaissance. The theory
of evolution, with its staggering picture of man's biological
development through millions of years from protoplasm to
homo sapiens, could not fail, despite its gaps, to impress the
mind with a sense of gradual but inexorable progress.
Science seemed to show mankind climbing slowly ever
upwards and onwards. Day by day and in every way man
was getting better and better. Hence the popular notion of
inevitable progress.

The facile equation of biological evolution with moral
progress was, of course, unwarranted and fallacious. But
Christians, somewhat bewildered by an account of the
origins of life so different from that of the Genesis parable,
were not as quick to realise this error as they might have
been, and in that failure lay the seeds of defection from the
authentic Christian Gospel.

If man has evolved morally as well as biologically, then
there is no such thing as a fall, unless it be a fall upwards.
Sin is no longer sin, but only imperfection; a gradually
diminishing inheritance from a primitive past, inevitably
destined to be overcome in time. Psychology promised to
accelerate the process. It now seemed impossible to believe
in original sin. It soon became equally impossible to
believe in redemption. If man is not ' in sin ', there is
nothing for him to be saved from. Christ could no longer
be regarded as Saviour, but only as Example and Teacher.
This process of dilution and denial was rationalised by a
critical scholarship, especially in Germany, which endeavoured
to show that the doctrines of atonement and salvation were
unwarranted Pauline additions to the simple life and teaching
of a Galilean prophet, whose divinity exceeded that of
other men only in degree. The Gospel was no longer
good news, but merely good advice. Small wonder,
then, that theology lost the intellectual initiative. Small
wonder, then, that, despite the missionary enthusiasm of

the minority, the Church as a whole lost her sense of mission, and that Christianity to-day is regarded popularly as a somewhat idealistic system of ethics.

Hitler has called this bluff. He is the catalytic agent of a process that was indeed inevitable, but which has now burst upon the world with overwhelming force. We have lived to see all the proud technical and scientific achievement of man turned to self-destruction. Modern man stands, like Frankenstein, aghast at the monster he has made, but unable to stop its career of torture and murder. We find ourselves caught in a vast vicious circle of evil. We are forced to kill and render homeless thousands of innocent women and children in Germany to save the remnants of civilisation. St. Paul's words, though used by him in a rather different context, exactly describe our condition, " The good that I would, I do not : the evil that I would not, that I do " (and must go on doing to the end), " O wretched man that I am ! " It is no longer possible to believe in man's ability to save himself from this contradictory condition by social amelioration and applied psychology. Even Professor C. E. M. Joad, who in the past has been no lover of Christian dogma, now recognises this. He writes :—

> " This belief " (in the power of man to banish the evil from society) " is no longer held with the old conviction. The fact is not surprising, since recent events have rendered it diminishingly plausible. It is extraordinarily difficult to believe that the beings who, as they go swaggering, oppressing, plundering, murdering, torturing and raping their way up and down the length and breadth of Europe, are giving one of the best exhibitions since the Thirty Years War of the stuff of which human nature is made, are *all* the victims, and *wholly* the victims, of unwise psychological

training and economic injustice. In other words, let evil be sufficiently obtrusive and sufficiently widespread, and let men's noses be rubbed in it with sufficient violence, and they will find it increasingly difficult to resist the belief that it is in the nature of the beast; that men, in short, are like that. And here we are back at the doctrine of original sin, of the conception of man as a creature whose heart is desperately wicked, with all the theological implications that the doctrine is apt to bring in its train." [1]

We are back, in fact, at the heart of the Gospel. Man needs redemption from sin. That such redemption has been wrought, and is available for mankind, is precisely what the Christian Gospel proclaims. The scales have fallen from our eyes. As Christians, we can again speak of Christ as Saviour. Though we stand in need of penitence that any of us should ever have ceased thus to speak, we can rejoice that we have recovered our Gospel. Indeed, nothing short of that Gospel can meet the condition of our rapidly disintegrating society.

But to recover our Gospel is one thing. To present it in such a way that our contemporaries can at least understand what we are talking about is another. There is much leeway to be made up. Having for a while lost sight of our Gospel, we have ceased to speak in prophetic accents, and we have therefore lost the ear of our generation. We cannot proceed with evangelism as if nothing had happened. Popular, liberal Christianity has bequeathed to us a heritage of widespread ignorance and confusion about the very elements of the Christian Faith. The problem thus presented is that of knowing where to begin. The answer commonly assumed is that, somehow or other, people must be brought *to church*. But since Church services are

[1] Quoted from *The New Statesman*, August 22nd, 1942.

designed to provide a vehicle for the worship of those who already accept the Christian Faith, it is inevitable that those who have not accepted that faith should find the language of authentic Christian worship almost wholly foreign. Hence arises the now common plea that Church services should be so modified and modernised as to 'attract' the people whom we desire to reach.

But this line of approach contains a quite fundamental difficulty. Belief (the *lex credendi*) and worship (the *lex orandi*) are so closely bound up together that they cannot be divorced without danger to both. It is inherently impossible to design a form of worship which will at one and the same time 'attract' the average modern man and provide a framework in which the authentic Christian Gospel can be preached. The one gives the lie to the other. The purpose of this book is to try to show why this must be so, and to suggest an alternative line of approach. Our first task, therefore, must be to make clear the grounds of the claim that the Church's belief cannot safely be separated from the Church's worship.

2. *The Evangel and the Liturgy.*

In point of fact and history the Church's worship is, and always has been, one of the Church's chief ways of proclaiming her Gospel. The evangel which the Anglican preacher is called to preach derives from a two-fold source, and is contained in a two-fold treasure-house. Their proper names are Dogma and Liturgy. To a generation riddled with 'points of view' and accustomed to measure all things by the yard-stick of individual experience, the first of these terms is so offensive as to call for some explanation.

Christians are sometimes reproached because they display less enthusiasm for their faith than do Communists for theirs. But what distinguishes the Christian from the Communist ' faith ' is not enthusiasm, but ' dogma '—*i.e.*, *revealed truth*. To say that the Church lives by dogma and liturgy is not to deny the need for personal religion. Dogma and liturgy are respectively the seed and soil in which alone the flower of personal devotion can grow and flourish. " Love so amazing, so divine, demands my life, my soul, my all." There speaks true personal religion. But whose or what is this so amazing love ? If the answer to this question rests on no authority outside the personal experience of the speaker, it cannot claim to be a gospel for all other men. The Christian Faith does not derive from the subjective experience of Christians (though the cumulative experience of Christians is a strong argument for its truth), but from the saving act of God in Christ, wrought out in the objective arena of human history. What is unique about the Christian Faith is its appeal to history. Its primary concern, however, is not with those facts as facts, but with their meaning.

No man is a Christian simply because he accepts the fact that a person called Jesus once lived and was put to death. To say that Jesus Christ " suffered under Pontius Pilate, was crucified, dead and buried ", is merely to state a fact of history which no self-respecting scholar or historian would dare to deny. But to add that this historic personage was " the only begotten Son of God . . . God of God, Light of Light, Very God of Very God " is to plunge headlong into dogma. But it is by this dogma, this interpretation of fact or revealed truth, that the Church lives. The Christian Faith is essentially dogmatic, as distinct from being empirical or experimental or mythical. " God so loved the world that he gave his only-begotten Son, that whosoever believeth in him should not perish, but have everlasting life " is sheer, unadulterated dogma. There can be no Christian Faith without it. Nor is the acceptance of such dogma the unreasoning credulity with which the word ' dogma ' has come unfortunately to be associated. It is not a theologian but a Professor of Mathematics who writes :—

" Belief in theological doctrines is, however, not necessarily any less rational than belief in the statements of natural philosophy : the doctrines of the Church are not vague or doubtful, as compared with the results of science, and the confidence is not less secure. Indeed, if religion were merely a matter of personal opinion or emotion, of conjectural rather than of reasoned conviction, it would be incapable of illumining and explaining in a larger setting the knowledge which has been gained by scientific research. To do this, it must be a corpus of definite and firmly held objective truth. Religions that have vital force and influence are positive religions : that is, religions with ordinances and dogmas. What are these dogmas ? Essentially they are the solutions of the great problems that have never ceased to engage and perplex the mind of man—the nature of reality, the existence of God, the origin of the world, the source of evil, the expiation of sin, the future of humanity. Dogma is the core of every system of faith and worship : without it, religion would dissolve into mere sentiment, and would, in a few generations, perish altogether." [1]

Christian dogma is the foundation on which the Christian religion rests. The Christian dogma is the Christian datum. It is to be noted that the words ' dogma ' and ' doctrine ' are not identical terms. ' Dogma ' is revealed truth. The word ' doctrine ' is normally used to signify

[1] Professor E. T. Whittaker, Riddell Memorial Lecture, *The Beginning and End of the World*, Oxford University Press, p. 5.

B

either (1) the attempt to formulate this truth in the language and idiom of a particular age or society or (2) truths which, though not ' revealed ', are implicit in or deducible from revelation.[1]

The importance of this distinction is seen when we ask, " How does the Church proclaim her Gospel or ' dogma ' ? " Partly by rationalising it into doctrines. All down the ages Christian preachers and teachers have expounded the great dogmas or facts of revealed truth in the thought-forms of their own age and society. But if this were the sole means of propagating and proclaiming Christian truth, there would be a grave risk of its passing away with the current intellectual fashion. Had the dogma of the Atonement been dependent on its doctrinal formulation by the School-men, it might long since have disappeared from enlightened thought. Christian dogma is preserved by the Apostles' and Nicene Creeds. They stand for all time as the authentic statement of revealed truth. But though the Creeds are instruments of preservation, they are not, nor were they ever intended to be, instruments of proclamation. The Creed is a statement of the Gospel. But to recite the Creed is not the same thing as to preach the Gospel. Apart from the spoken word of the preacher, the Church has another instrument by which she proclaims her Gospel or dogma ; that is the Liturgy.[2]

Through the centuries Christians have expressed their faith in certain actions and words addressed to God, of which actions and words the two gospel-sacraments, Baptism and the Lord's Supper, are the chief. The liturgy is dogma

---

[1] This distinction is not always maintained—e.g., we speak of the ' doctrine ' of the Incarnation. It would perhaps be more exact to speak of the ' dogma ' of the Incarnation. It is, however, correct to speak of the ' doctrine ' rather than the ' dogma ' of the Real Presence at the Eucharist.

[2] Hereafter a capital ' L' will be used only to refer to the Liturgy proper (i.e., the Eucharistic Rite), as distinct from the whole body of liturgical worship and actions, spoken of as liturgy.

given worshipful and objective expression. Through the church building, its furniture and appointments, through the regular round of sacraments and services, rites and ceremonies, the Church proclaims the truth by which she lives. Here is not doctrine, but dogma. Here is no argument or rationalisation, only doing. We are not invited to consider the evidence for the existence of God. We are caught up in worship. There is no attempt to explain just in what ways prayer is fundamentally different from autosuggestion. We are invited to join our prayers with those of the whole Church. We are not asked to compare alternative theories of the Atonement, or to speculate upon the problem of suffering. We are bidden in the breaking of bread to shew forth the Lord's death till he come.

> " By the influence of the Church service the regular
> Church people are moulded ; for the things which they
> do in church make a deeper impression than the teach-
> ing which reaches their minds. Often they have
> thought that they came to church chiefly to hear the
> sermon. This, however, they mostly forgot ; but
> there were responses and prayers, commandments,
> creeds and scriptures, which impressed themselves on
> their mind by constant repetition. All these things,
> the church building and the ritual and the ceremonies
> which take place in it, speak of the reality of God
> after a manner different in kind from the exhortations
> and instructions of the preacher." [1]

If you want to know what the Church believes, study her worship.[2] Preachers may present partial and personalist

---

[1] A. G. Hebert, *Liturgy and Society*, p. 39. This book is an important and scholarly exposition of the whole subject.

[2] This truth was most impressively demonstrated at the Amsterdam Youth Conference of 1939, each member of which was enabled to enter sympathetically into the genius of Christian traditions other than his own by sharing in their worship. The Con-

versions of the Gospel. The lives of individual Christians may bear but feeble witness to their faith. But look at the Church's corporate liturgical actions and modes of expression; examine over a period of several hundred years her prayer-books and sacraments, her rites and ceremonies, and you will be brought face to face with the Truth by which she lives.

Since the Church's liturgy derives from and proclaims her Gospel, any conception of evangelism which ignores the liturgy is not only depriving itself of one of its most effective instruments, but also runs a grave risk of partial and doctrinaire lop-sidedness. It is significant that the liberal attempt to produce a theology consistent with the philosophy of inevitable progress, issued in a form of religious exercises, popularised by some preachers and broadcasters in the years between the wars, which are as far removed in thought and language from traditional Christian worship as chalk is from cheese. Decline in the content of dogma involves decline in the standard of worship and vice versa. Hence the danger of trying to attract those outside the Church with bowdlerised forms of worship.[1]

The Liturgical Movement, which began in the Roman Church on the Continent, and has attracted some attention in England, has arisen to recall the Church to the primacy of worship in her corporate life, and to its importance as a means of presenting the Gospel of our redemption. But there has been little conscious attempt to relate worship to the task of evangelism. That there are some to whom

---

ference ' daily service ' was taken by people of different countries according to the tradition they represented. Thus, the service on one morning was according to the Order of the French Reformed Church, on another it was an African Free Church service, on another there was a celebration of the Orthodox Liturgy, and so on.

[1] Compare the two following prayers from *When Two or Three* (compiled for use at the daily Broadcast Services) with those from the B.C.P., which in each case are printed on the same page in this book.

liturgy, especially the Liturgy proper, comes as an evangelistic challenge is shown by the following incident. The

---

When Two or Three, p. 24.

O God of Love, who art in all places and times, pour thy
spirit of healing and comfort upon every lonely heart. Have
pity upon those who are bereft of human love, and on those to
whom it has never come. Grant unto them to know the love
of the Heavenly Father, and in the end give them fulness of
joy for the sake of Jesus Christ our Lord.

WITH

From B.C.P.

Almighty and everlasting God, mercifully look upon our
infirmities, and in all our dangers and necessities stretch forth
thy right hand to help and defend us ; through Jesus Christ
our Lord.

AND

When Two or Three, pp. 30–31.

O God, our Heavenly Father, we thy children come now
before thee with our supplications. We cannot live without
thy blessing. Life is too hard for us, duty is too large. We
get discouraged and are too easily disheartened. We come to
thee in our weakness, asking thee for strength. Help us always
to be of good cheer. Let us not be dismayed by our difficulties.
Let us never doubt thy love or thy promises. Give us grace
to be encouragers of others, never discouragers. Let us not go
about with sadness or fear among men, but let us always make
life easier, never harder, for those who come within our
influence, and help us to show something of the love of Christ
in our lives. We beseech thee to hear us, to receive our prayer,
and to forgive our sins ; for the sake of Jesus Christ.

WITH

From B.C.P.

We humbly beseech thee, O Father, mercifully to look upon
our infirmities, and for the glory of thy name turn from us all
those evils that we most righteously have deserved, and grant
that in all our troubles we may put our whole trust and
confidence in thy mercy, and evermore serve thee in holiness
and pureness of living, to thine honour and glory ; through
our only Mediator and Advocate, Jesus Christ our Lord.

The difference is not merely one of language, but of theology.
The ' modern ' prayers put the emphasis on man, his needs and
difficulties, and seem to suggest that all that is needed is a little
help and uplift from God to make human life happy and beneficent.
The Prayer Book prayers put the emphasis, rightly, upon God and

priest-in-charge of a seaside church, where the parish communion is well established, was accosted after the celebration on Sunday morning by a young barrister who said, " I should like to have a talk with you. I must explain that this is the first time I have been in a church since I was married. But being on holiday, and with nothing else to do, I came here this morning with my wife. I don't in the least understand what this service is all about, but I have been forced to realise that these people have been *doing* something which is to them of vital importance. It has been an entirely new experience for me, and I'd like to know more about it."

But for every one who by some happy chance finds himself confronted by the challenge of Christians really at worship, a hundred pass the church doors in ignorance that anything of tremendous importance is going on inside. While the multitude is ignorant of Christian truth it is likely to remain uninfluenced by Christian worship. So long as it is out of contact with Christian worship it will never be brought face to face with the deepest Christian truth. Here is a vicious circle. The purpose of this book is to suggest a point at which this vicious circle may be broken. At first sight it may seem that the point chosen, and the method suggested, are in direct opposition to the truth outlined above, and involve a reversal of the process by which a man learns Christian truth by taking part in Christian worship. But since in this rationalist and self-sufficient

---

His mercy. There is full recognition of the sinfulness of man, and of man's powerlessness to achieve good except by God's grace. I suggest that a bomber pilot (upon whom our civilisation has laid such an awful necessity of scattering death and destruction) could pray the Prayer Book prayers. He would find it hard to repeat the words of the ' modern ' prayers without ribaldry or blasphemy.

Note.—This book was first published in 1932, and is quoted as illustrative of the tendencies of the popular religious devotions of the period. The above is NOT intended to imply any criticism of the present staff of the Religious Department of the B.B.C.

age the majority of people cannot be persuaded to take part in Christian worship at all, let alone approach it with the humility that is willing to learn anything from it, may it not be that they can be initiated into Christian worship *as part of their instruction in the Christian Faith*? I believe that they can. I believe that some at least of the people at present outside our churches can be approached first on the level of Christian dogma. But unless they are at the same time initiated into Christian worship, the supernatural truth of the faith will never become translated into supernatural living.

But I wish to emphasise that I regard the method of approach about to be described as one which, since it is designed to meet the needs of this generation, may well become outmoded or unnecessary in thirty or forty years time. Indeed, if its purpose could be achieved on any considerable scale, it would have rendered itself superfluous, since the children of those who have been initiated into the worshipping community will be born and bred in liturgy. Until that blessed day dawns, something of the kind of technique outlined in the following pages will, I believe, be necessary.

CHAPTER I

THE PRESENT SITUATION

AN official of the B.B.C. once remarked that one of the essential precautions for a broadcast preacher to observe is the avoidance of technical terms. " If," he said, " a man were to begin a broadcast sermon by saying, ' To-day, my friends, is Septuagesima,' about fifty thousand sets would at once be switched off ! " There is in this country to-day an increasingly wide gulf between those who have been brought up in the tradition of Christian thought and observance, and those who have not. Among the latter, who constitute by far the larger section of the community, Christian terminology is either devoid of meaning, as is the case with such words as ' Redemption ', 'Atonement ', and ' Grace ', or is completely misunderstood, as in the case of such terms as ' Sin ', ' Faith ', ' Prayer ', and even the word ' Christian ' itself. A contributor to a recent issue of *The Christian News-Letter* made the following indictment :

> " The terminology of Christian worship and popular theology is understood by many clergy, though few interpret it to their congregations. To many older people, brought up in the traditions of a Church, it is sacred and dear, but for many of these its familiarity obscures and distorts its meaning. To the ears of those outside the Church, ' unfamiliar with religious vocabulary ', much of the terminology sounds either meaningless or contemptible. To very many churchgoers what they hear in Church has only the soothing effect of incantation. Outsiders ' ready to respond to the Christian message ' but uninstructed in the meaning of our terminology, go away complaining that Christianity is

anthropomorphic, polytheistic and materialistic—either blasphemy or nonsense." [1]

Faced by this alarming situation there is a tendency on the part of many Christians to look round for some immediate remedy, some bold step which, if it will not lead to the conversion of the masses, will at least stop the rot and prevent the situation from degenerating further. What more natural therefore than to say " Let us have brighter and more modern services, services that are relevant to the lives that people have to live. Why stick to old-fashioned language that no one can understand "? Even among clergy one sometimes hears the desire expressed for forms of service which are either alternatives to or modifications of the Prayer Book offices of Morning and Evening Prayer and which will meet the needs of those who, having been long out of touch with corporate worship, find these services beyond their understanding.

It is, however, of the utmost importance that any such steps should be taken with a very clear idea, not only of the immediate need they are designed to meet, but also of the ultimate objective to be achieved. Nor must we omit to ask whether that objective will best be achieved by the provision of forms of service, however modified and however modern. Let us begin by considering this obvious difficulty of language.

Let it be granted that though the use of technical terms is a convenience and an aid to accurate expression in religion, as in chemistry, mathematics or philosophy, a working grasp of the Christian religion is not necessarily dependent upon familiarity with its specialised vocabulary. Christianity claims to be a universal religion. It claims to be equally appropriate to the first-century Palestinian Jew, the third-century Roman soldier, the mediaeval serf and the modern statesman. Now, if this claim is true, it follows that there

[1] *The Christian News-Letter*, March 4th, 1942.

must be a way of translating the basic truths of the Christian Gospel into the language of every man in every circumstance.

It does not, of course, follow that these truths will be accepted. There will always be those to whom the preaching of the Cross seems either foolish or offensive. But it is implicit in the universal claim of the Christian Gospel that it is capable of being made clear to all men in all ages. Neither does it follow that technical terms can be wholly dispensed with in religion, any more than they can in other branches of thought. It does mean, however, that they are capable of approximate translation into the language of current speech. The fact that many people will not grant to religion the same right to possess its own language as they will concede to the physical or social sciences, let alone approach the former with the same patience and humility that they will willingly give to the latter, is evidence of the curious irrationality which characterises the popular modern attitude towards religion. Though one would have thought that words like ' atonement ', ' grace ' or ' faith ' were much less terrifying to the eye and repugnant to the ear than such terms as ' psycho-physical parallelism ', ' schizo-phrenia ' or ' dialectical materialism ' ! Be that as it may, the need for a modern presentation of the Christian religion which does not presuppose a previous acquaintance with Christian terminology is evident.

But the meeting of this need is the task of the Christian writer, teacher and evangelist, and one that is being undertaken with considerable ability by several well-known writers and many lesser-known clergy and teachers. The outstanding genius of Miss Dorothy L. Sayers and the acumen and wit of Mr. C. S. Lewis are of inestimable value to the Christian cause, and what these writers are doing for a section of the thoughtful reading public many priests and pastors are doing in a humbler way for some of the less enlightened and non-reading members of the community.

All this work of translation and interpretation is necessary in every age. Would that many more clergy were alive to the need both of talking in plain but not slovenly English in the pulpit and also of giving much more of their attention to the fundamental truths of the Christian Creed.

It does not, however, follow that what is true of the necessity of non-theological and up-to-date language in books, lectures and sermons addressed to those outside the small circle of ' the faithful ' applies with equal force to Christian worship. On the contrary, Christian worship presupposes a congregation of people who have come together for the express purpose of worshipping God in response to and in the setting of His historic Incarnation and sacrificial death. Without an acceptance of these truths Christian worship as such cannot begin. Moreover, since the knowledge of, and supernatural grace deriving from, Christ's Incarnation and Atonement are mediated to us through a divinely appointed society which is both ageless and universal in character, and since Christians worship together not as individuals but as members of this trans-historic society, it would be inappropriate and unnatural if the language of Christian worship were drawn merely or chiefly from contemporary sources.

To the hypothetical (some would say mythical!) outsider ' ready to respond to the Christian message but uninstructed in the meaning of our terminology ' there is a perfectly legitimate answer. Why should he *expect* that the language of Christian worship should be intelligible to one who rarely shares in it ? He would probably be even more bewildered by a Masonic ceremony if he could be an invisible spectator. But though he might think that Masons were odd people, he would not complain because he did not understand what they were talking about. He would grant them the right to be peculiar. There is an important sense in which the same right should be conceded to Christians at worship. To offer worship to

God in this scientifically-minded and self-sufficient age is to be peculiar, and the ' outsider ' has no real grounds for complaint because the language of Christian worship is unfamiliar or even meaningless to his uninitiated ear.

Even if some genius could re-write the traditional forms of Christian worship in language which was at once dignified and simple, and yet did not depend for its significance upon the possession of a Christian culture, there is another difficulty which the ' outsider ' would encounter. Any form of worship must be based upon some dogmatic foundations or presuppositions. Traditional Christian worship derives from the truths contained in the Nicene and Apostles' Creeds. But very many of those who are sympathetic to what they believe to be the ethical ideals of Christianity are not at all convinced that its dogmatic foundations are either true or necessary for a promulgation of its ethics. Their attitude is exactly expressed in the words of the following question recently addressed to the writer during the course of a Christian Brains-Trust.

> " Many people to-day are prepared to accept Christ's teaching, but they are unable to accept the doctrine of his divinity. Does this matter ? Surely the core and essence of Christianity is the Sermon on the Mount. Why, then, does the Church insist on doctrines which no one can understand and which do not affect the practical implications of loving one's neighbour as oneself ? "

What ' form of service ' could be devised to express such nebulous humanitarianism as this ? " Well," says the advocate of reform, " cannot this ethical idealism be dedicated to God ? " Surely it can. But to what kind of a God ? To a God " who for us men and for our salvation came down from heaven and was incarnate ", or to one who did not ? Such an exercise, if devised, could certainly not be described as ' Christian ', and it is doubtful if it could be called worship.

It will be convenient at this point to analyse the situation a little more carefully. Broadly speaking, and with all due precaution against the dangers of generalisation, each of the two classes of the community ' The Churchgoers ' and ' The Non-Churchgoers ' may be subdivided thus :

A.   THE CHURCHGOERS.

1. The minority of religiously educated Christians who accept the obligations and discipline of conscious member-ship in a worshipping community.

2. The majority of people who, though much more loosely attached to the Church, and often vague and ill-instructed in their understanding of the Christian Faith, yet count themselves part of the Christian community and are familiar with its language and worship.

B.   THE NON-CHURCHGOERS.

1. Those who, while not unsympathetic towards, are woefully ignorant of, the Christian Faith and are in despair at the apparent unreadiness of the Churches to translate their terminology into a language understood of the people. For the most part they have not consciously accepted the Incarnation because they have not been led to appreciate either its significance or its centrality.

2. Those who have come to the conclusion that the Christian religion is so hopelessly irrelevant that they are completely indifferent and impervious to any overtures made in their direction.

3. Those who have decided that Christianity is either false or a barrier to progress, and who have embraced one of the many modern substitutes, political or religious.

4. Those who have neither the desire nor the ability to think seriously about life at all.

Now, it is clear that by whatever ways the Church may be able to discharge her evangelistic responsibility to the people in categories B2, B3 and B4, it cannot be by the provision of 'forms of service'! It sometimes happens that circumstances may throw any of these folk into contact with Christians the supernatural quality of whose lives or the intellectual championship of whose convictions constitutes an inescapable challenge. But though the antagonistic are greatly to be preferred to the indifferent (indeed, an exterior antagonism often hides a deeper desire to be convinced), we must grant to every responsible being the right to say " No ", provided that we have done our best to see that he does at least understand what it is that he is rejecting. In any case, whatever advances may be made to these people, it will not be by way of services, however simplified, because they will not come to them.

In the case of those in the category A2 there is no acute need for the provision of modified or modernised forms of service. Though there is much to be done in a pastoral way to bring them more fully into the life and worship of the Church, they are prepared to accept that worship as the standard because they are familiar with it. Though many of them find occasional simplified non-liturgical services ' helpful ', they would soon find a regular diet of such services poverty-stricken and unsatisfactory by comparison with the traditional forms to which they are accustomed. Their need is not the provision of new forms, but rather some real training in their appreciation and use of the old ones. It is presumably those who are classified as B1 whose needs the advocates of revised and modified services and concerned to meet. But since a considerable proportion, probably the majority, of these non-churchgoing people have not accepted the basic truth of the Incarnation, it is difficult to see how they can take part in a Christian service, however simplified, without compromising their integrity. Moreover, it is certainly not the Church's job to provide non-Christian services of worship.

It may be replied that such people do, in point of fact, come occasionally to church for a special service, as *e.g.* on a Day of National Prayer, and are helped and uplifted. But helped to do what? Uplifted where? Are they thereby brought any nearer to an acceptance of the Christian religion? Evidence does not seem to show that they are. Indeed, the thoughtless reiteration of truths which people do not really believe or of prayers that presuppose an acceptance of those truths is not strengthening but weakening to the character. Moreover, for the Church to become a purveyor of mere popular uplift is not only to compromise with her super-natural Gospel, but also to run a grave risk of alienating those souls who have a real integrity and who are merely sickened by cheap sentimentality. There would appear to be only one legitimate reason for desiring that those who, however sympathetic to Christian ethics, have not accepted the Christian Faith should be present at a ' service ', and that is that they may possibly learn something of Christian truth from the sermon. But why in order to listen to an exposition of the Christian Faith should those who have not embraced that faith be expected to share in a service of Christian worship? There is every reason why they should not.

In the days now gone, when the majority of people were familiar with the fundamental truths of the Christian religion, the problem did not arise. But now a new situation has arisen in which a considerable section of the population, though willing, many of them, to listen to an exposition of Christian truth, have an insufficient grasp of that truth to make Christian worship an intelligent and significant activity.

If and when such people desire further information they have every right to complain that the only regular and local provision of such instruction is within the setting of a liturgical service which presupposes a background of Christian culture and belief that they may be seeking but to which they have not yet attained.   This may partly account for the fact that very few of such people ever think of going to church to seek such enlightenment.   They may read books, or listen to broadcast talks, or discuss religious topics with friends who are frequently as ill informed as they are themselves.   Should such a ' seeker ' enter the doors of a church he has no legitimate cause for complaint because the Church's Sunday worship is beyond his comprehension.   He has, however, a perfect right to complain that no instruction is provided apart from the setting of worship.   But even where there has been adequate instruction in and acceptance of the great truths of the Christian Faith, there will still be need for training in the art of worship.   In this pragmatic and self-sufficient age worship does not come easy to those who have some real knowledge of God.   It is practically impossible for those with little or none.   For the vast majority of people in this country *worship must be preceded by instruction, and instruction must be followed by training in worship.*

We have to face the fact that there is a wide gulf between those who are within the liturgical tradition and practice of Christian worship and those who are outside it.   But the parochial system provides no kind of bridge by which people may pass from the one company into the other.   What is needed is a kind of ' half-way house ', to which people may come if they wish, for enlightenment as to what the Christian religion is, but which does not demand of them the standard or obligations of full Church membership.   We need, in fact, to make room for a real *Catechumenate.*[1]

---

[1] It may be argued that since in the early Church the function of the Catechumenate was to prepare people for Baptism, a use of the term to describe the training of people, many of whom were baptised in infancy, is incorrect.   But in so far as we contemplate bringing them to a ratification of their baptismal vows (or in some cases to Confirmation) the term may perhaps be allowed.

Such a suggestion may seem to some presumptuous or pedantic. They will point to the undoubtedly Christian spirit displayed by great numbers of our fellow-countrymen in the present crisis, to their readiness to undertake exacting tasks without grumbling, to give of their best without thought of self and to show great cheerfulness and courage in the face of danger and misfortune. That these qualities partake of Christ's spirit is not to be denied, and there is no doubt but that he approves them. But to take an honest part in Christian worship presupposes not only the possession of certain Christian qualities, but also a recognition of him from whom they come. The common identification of Christian ethics and the display of the Christian ' spirit ' with the Christian religion is based on ignorance of the true nature of that religion. Witness the vast numbers of people who imagine that this war is being waged for ' Christianity '. It is true that we are fighting for justice, freedom and the preservation of the dignity and worth of the individual. But these virtues and ideals are not peculiarly ' Christian '. They are ' Natural '. They belong to man as man. That is why Russians who are Marxian atheists can fight for them with passionate sincerity. The Christian virtues are more than, and go beyond the natural virtues. They are strictly *supernatural*. The specifically Christian virtues are faith, hope and charity, and though the Christian religion cannot flourish in a society in which the natural virtues are denied, the Christian religion is supernatural because it has come from beyond this world. It is not the result of man having said " By what principles and ideals can we make a more satisfactory world ? " The Christian religion is the result of God having said " Behold thou shalt conceive in thy womb and bring forth a son . . . and shalt call his name Jesus, for he shall save his people from their sins ".

It is the Church's solemn duty both to God and to man to preserve the integrity and the supernatural nature of the

c

Christian religion. To invite people to join in popular and simple 'services' the theological presuppositions and implications of which have been tempered to the measure of their unbelief is not only to deny the essential Christian Gospel, but to fail them at their point of deepest need. The demand for shorter and simpler services may be all right if it is directed against unnecessary long-windedness and cheap sentimental music. But if (as in some cases there is reason to believe) it is an attempt to gloss over the sterner side of man's sins and God's claims with Pelagian exuberance of the 'gallant and high-hearted happiness' variety, it is all wrong. There is a very grave danger that in setting out to 'meet people's needs' we end by offering them religion on man's terms rather than on God's. It is significant that most of the experiments in the field of popular religion in the Church of England have been associated with that Liberal Modernist theology which makes religion agreeable by emptying it almost entirely of its supernatural and dogmatic content; witness some of the hymns in *Songs of Praise*. The danger that besets the laudable attempt to provide 'milk for babes' is that the milk may become so diluted in the process that it would not be recognised as such by any self-respecting cow.

An example of this tendency may be found in the 'Form of National Prayer and Dedication issued for the third anniversary of the outbreak of War'. Presumably it was felt that the language of the General Confession was too strong. So, instead, we were invited to acknowledge that " we had not loved God with all our hearts ". (Who has ?) " That we had not loved our neighbours as ourselves " (which is perhaps just as well); but anyway we were not quite perfect yet, so we prayed " Help us to overcome our faults ". Now, there is a good deal to be said for the occasional use of this 1928 form of Confession. But in the circumstances of a

National Day of Prayer, with European civilisation toppling in ruins, and when, if ever, we ought to be thinking seriously about how human history must appear to God, such under-statement of man's sin is almost a falsification of truth.

This particular illustration may not be, perhaps, a very happy one, as it may appear to some to be controvertible, and certainly calls for fuller treatment than is possible here. But it will serve as a pointer to the many pitfalls that lie in the path of those who are conscious of their Christian responsi-bility to the great unchurched, and particularly of those who try to meet this responsibility by the provision of ' suitable ' forms of worship. That there has been, and still is, a tendency in some quarters to water down the great Biblical truths of man's fallen state and his need of redemption, and to substitute a doctrine of salvation by works for that of justification by faith is all too evident. This is not the cry of a reactionary or a pedant. We have to choose between theo-centric and supernatural religion (and the authentic Gospel is both), and that thinly-veiled humanism which so often passes for ' Christianity '. We shall do grave disservice to the former by over-simplification, rationalisation and understatement of revealed truth. Nor is it the way by which souls are won. As Mr. D. R. Davies says : " Modern man sees no necessity for a Church which merely dresses his own egotism in a religious garb. Though he will understand less, he will be more impressed and challenged by a faith radically different from his own." [1]

What we should say to the ' sympathetic outsider ' is not : " You find our services dull and their language unintelligible ? Then we will overhaul them so that their language is up to date and remove from them any theological beliefs that you do not at present hold."

What we should say in effect is : " You find our services

[1] D. R. Davies, *On to Orthodoxy*, p. 179.

incomprehensible and their language unintelligible? That is not surprising, since it is the language of an age-less Church beside which even the British Empire is a parvenu, and since it speaks of great mysteries of which modern people are for the most part ignorant, and which they are not very ready to accept. Therefore, though we should be glad to welcome you into our fellowship and to a share in our worship, we realise that you must first know exactly what it is we believe and what we presuppose in our worship. We will accordingly offer you an opportunity to familiarise yourself with our faith, and to ask all the questions that you want to ask. Then we must give you time to decide whether or not you are prepared to accept this faith. If you are not, then we respect your decision. If you are, then we will offer you a further opportunity to learn and to practise the art of worshipping God, which we believe to be the true end of man."

It is frequently said that conditions in this country approximate increasingly to those of the mission field. In so far as those conditions are a Christian minority and a largely pagan majority, that is true, but with one very important difference. Whereas the pagans overseas can consider the Christian faith with an open mind because it is to them entirely new and radically different from anything they have ever heard before, the pagans at home think they know what Christianity is already, and they come to it (when they come) with minds that have been side-tracked by identification of the Christian Gospel with humanitarian ethics.

In the mission-field no would-be Christian is allowed to take his full part in Christian worship until he has served his catechumenate, has given evidence of the reality of his conversion and has been baptised. The circumstances of this country to-day make some sort of training-stage or catechumenate even more necessary, for though very many of our people were baptised as infants, they have either denied or failed to implement the vows made on their behalf by their god-parents, and are, in vast numbers of cases, ignorant of what these vows presuppose and involve.

CHAPTER II

THE CATECHUMENATE

I

WE have contended that the present religious condition of this country calls for the revival of a training-stage or catechumenate. But it would obviously be impossible to envisage in detail all that such a fundamental and far-reaching change in our technique would involve. Such a catechumenate would grow from small beginnings and local experiments. It could not be devised as a theoretical blueprint ready made for immediate application. Indeed, the many local attempts now being made to reach those outside the small circle of the faithful indicate a growing awareness of the need for something analogous to the catechumenate, and are slowly feeling towards it. It will be our business to notice and describe some of these experiments and to suggest further developments along similar lines. But before we pass on to do this, there is one criticism that must first be met, and the answer to which will clarify some of the issues involved.

There may be some who will say, " Surely the Anglican Church already possesses a catechumenate. The element of responsible personal decision which the ancient catechumenate provided is furnished by the rite of Confirmation in which those who have been baptised in infancy take upon themselves the promises made by their god-parents on their behalf." In theory this is true. In practice it has largely broken down, because the conditions envisaged by the Prayer Book no longer exist. The Prayer Book quite clearly contemplates the Confirmation of children who are being brought up in Christian homes and within the framework of a Christian society. It assumes that all " Fathers, Mothers, Masters and Dames shall cause their Children, Servants and Prentices, (which have not learned their Catechism) to come to the Church at the time appointed " (*i.e.*, after the second lesson at Evensong) " and obediently to hear, and be ordered by the Curate, until such time as they have learned all that is . . . appointed for them to learn ",[1] and as soon as they are come to a competent age they shall be brought to the Bishop to be confirmed. In such circumstances the Confirmation of young adolescents was, humanly speaking, a comparatively safe affair, since the influence and practice of their homes and the judgments of contemporary society tended to help them towards, rather than to militate against, the implementing of their Christian vows. To say this is not to suggest that the England that gave birth to the Prayer Book was a wholly Christian England. But at least God was revered as God, and sin was recognised as sin. If a man decided upon an evil course of action he did so with a full knowledge of its sinfulness. The Christian doctrines of the sovereignty of God and the creatureliness of man were accepted and implicit in social life.

But the boys and girls of today are living in such a wholly different world that the Confirmation of children, which was safe enough when the practice grew up, has, in the temper of modern society, become precarious in the extreme. There is no longer even a probability that the home will be Christian. The pull of the immediate environment of work, business, cinema, newspapers and of society as a whole is against, not towards, the practice of religion. In many cases we are placing on these boys and girls an almost intolerable strain by expecting them to choose between two ways of life and two sets of values, for the appreciation of one of which they are ill equipped by education and experience, and the other of which pulls at them all day and every day.

Few will deny that our present practice is not justified by

[1] Second Rubric after the Catechism, B.C.P.

results. Let the reader think of any parish that he has known for the past ten years. How many of the boys and girls who have been prepared for Confirmation and have been confirmed during that time are now regular communicant members of the Church? Twenty per cent? Ten per cent? Five per cent? In most cases it is less than five per cent. We are, in fact, creating every year large numbers of lapsed communicants. For this failure the clergy are not wholly, or even chiefly to blame. Most parish priests take considerable pains over the preparation of their candidates, and though the most important part of the work—viz., the after-care—is frequently overlooked, there is clearly something wrong with a system the results of which are so pathetically disproportionate to the labour expended. We are asking the impossible, both from the clergy and from their candidates.

This is all the more regrettable since the chief remedy lies in our own hands—namely, a revision of our ideas about the age at which, under the conditions of modern society, young men and women can be considered to have attained years of discretion sufficient for making the choice involved. This is not necessarily an argument for the postponement of Confirmation as such. It is a plea for the deferring of the ratification of Baptismal vows.

As at present practised by the Church of England, Confirmation involves two important acts: (1) the solemn ratification of Baptismal vows, and (2) admission to the sacrament of Holy Communion. These are two quite distinct things, and it is questionable whether, even in the case of those who have been brought up in a worshipping community, they ought to be coincident. The average boy or girl of fifteen is no more capable of making a life vow than is a child of ten or eleven. If in the conditions of contemporary society the ratification of Baptismal vows is to be a significant personal decision and not a meaningless farce, it should be deferred until sufficient stability of character and sufficient appreciation of life's larger issues have been achieved to make such a decision possible. This would not be before eighteen, and might well be several years later.

Yet one would not wish so long to deprive those who have been brought up in a Christian home and as a member of a worshipping community of the grace of the sacrament. From the point of view of admission to Holy Communion the sooner boys and girls can be admitted consistent with sufficient grasp of its significance the better. The earlier a habit is formed the greater its chances of persistence. The experience of those parishes where it is the custom to have children confirmed at the age of ten or eleven years would seem to emphasise the wisdom of early admission to communicant life, but it still leaves unsolved this further problem.

However good the religious education of a boy or girl has been, such education is by its very nature inadequate to the needs of adult life. The most cogent considerations, drawn both from psychology and from practical experience, go to show that whatever is ' learned ' during life's earlier and immature stages has to be re-assimilated during later years, or it has not been ' learned ' at all. Herein lies the fallacy in assuming that what has been taught to the young in schools or in Confirmation classes has been taught for ever. This truth is very succinctly expressed in the following words of Dr. J. H. Oldham, writing in the *Christian News-Letter*:

" One who is at present working in a large boys' club in London told me a few days ago that he had been much concerned by the seemingly complete ignorance of the basic facts of the Christian religion displayed by the vast majority of his boys. He visited the headmaster of a local elementary school from which many of these boys came, and found him not, as he had expected, apathetic about religious instruction, but really keen.

No teacher in this school was compelled to teach scripture, but none had refused : yet to the boys it was a school subject only, of no practical relevance, and left behind like a sloughed skin when they left school.

" I was once present at a conference of headmasters of public schools on the subject of religious education. It was agreed that religious conditions in the schools themselves were in the main satisfactory ; a large proportion of boys were genuinely interested in the scripture teaching and valued the Chapel services— religion met with a real response. There was similar agreement that in the majority the effects seemed to wear off altogether after they left school. This illustration from the public schools is important, because religious education is given under far more favourable conditions than we can expect to attain through the national system as a whole.

" Had the club organiser whose experience I have quoted been discussing English history instead of Bible knowledge with his boys, he would almost certainly have found that the facts they remembered were of the burnt-cakes order of importance. *It is exceedingly difficult to remember facts which are not relevant to experience.* (Italics mine. G. W. I.) At fourteen years old nearly nine out of ten of our nation's children leave school, where life has on the whole been based on consideration for others, honesty and truthfulness and fair play, and plunge into a world which regards these values as superfluous if they stand in the way of getting on. The more the school has been to the boy or girl a real community, the greater is the plunge into the working world. If worship and religious knowledge have never been brought into a child's life by anything but the school, it is only to be expected that they will be forgotten as irrelevant or even despised as unreal when he finds himself in a world which reverses most of the values which he has been taught to admire. The value of the scripture lesson is that it supplements the teaching of home and church and sets religious knowledge in the context of knowledge as a whole. When we look to it to convey the whole of religious experience we are asking for the impossible." [1]

The truth contained in the above quotation is not confined to the religious teaching given *in schools* only, but applies to almost all teaching given to the young and immature. There is a sense in which all religious teaching given to children is irrelevant, not to their lives as they are now, but to the lives they will have to live in ten years time. The probability is that during a boy's adolescence the religion of childhood will either become more peculiarly and significantly his own, or will be cast off with other childish things. Hitherto he has accepted the comparatively stable background provided by his home and school. At fourteen he is flung out into the economic market, and the props that have previously supported him are taken away. He has to find his own level in a larger and more complex environment. He has to come to terms with life and to choose what values and standards he will make his own. The values and standards which before he had accepted without question are reviewed in the light of larger experience and amid a variety of new influences. It is not surprising that the worldly-wise youth of nineteen, looking back on his Confirmation at fourteen, should feel that the promises he then made are no longer significant to or binding upon him. That many young folk do so regard their Confirmation vows was brought home to the writer by the following experience.

During the last six or seven years I have assisted in the

[1] *The Christian News-Letter*, March 17th, 1943.

formation of quite a number of parochial youth fellowships in a variety of parishes in different parts of England. The invitation to form such a fellowship has always been set against the larger background of God's great redemptive acts in a world adrift, and the fellowship has always been represented as a tiny section of the Church which Christ created to be the extension of his Incarnation. Yet in the majority of cases where the idea has been accepted and the fellowship formed there has been a demand for an admission service, and the following dialogue has repeatedly taken place.

> I. "Admission service? What for? The fellowship is only a part of the Church, and most of you have been confirmed, and are therefore members of the Church already. You can't be made members all over again."
>
> They. "Yes, but *it didn't mean anything then*. It would now. *Now* we understand what we are doing."

There is a strong case for the separation of the two elements of Confirmation as at present administered, in order that those boys and girls who are already part of a worshipping community may be admitted to the sacrament of Holy Communion as early as is wise in particular cases, but that Christian vows may be undertaken at a later and more responsible age. However well candidates are prepared for Confirmation during early adolescence, they will need a further period of intensive training in adult life—something over and above what is provided by sermons and instructions in the normal course of church-going. The first point I wish to establish is that whatever of religious truth is learned in childhood needs to be re-learned later. The second point to be made clear is that it must be re-learned in *a different way*.

This difference may best be made clear by an elementary consideration of the psychology involved. Viewed psychologically, religion is primarily an experience or series of experiences, resulting in a cultivated ' sentiment ' or attitude of mind. Neither religious experience nor the religious attitude of mind can be conveyed from one person to another by instruction. They are communicable, so to say, by infection. This is the truth in the saying " Religion is caught rather than taught ". But religious experience, like any other type of experience, in order to be of significance to the mind, needs to be interpreted, and for this purpose of interpretation it is necessary to be in possession of the right and relevant facts. Where this knowledge is lacking or inaccurate the interpretation will be wrong. For example, the man of the ancient world experienced the somewhat terrifying noise and lightning of a thunderstorm, and said to himself, " God must be very angry ". The modern interpretation of the same experience into terms of electrical discharge results from the possession of knowledge of the physical universe of which the ancients were ignorant. Hence the necessity of religious knowledge for religion.

Our minds have in this connection a two-fold function, just as our bodies have in the matter of food. One bodily function is the masticating or ' taking in ' of food. There follows a further process by which that food is digested and translated into terms of energy and heat. So with our minds. One function of the mind ' takes in ' experience. Another function translates or ' interprets ' it.[1] However direct and awe-inspiring may be a man's experience of God, that experience has still to be interpreted by his mind. That is why it is important that his mind should be enlightened by right religious knowledge. In pre-Christian days men interpreted the sense of God's power in terms of a bull or of a great king ' high and lifted up '. But never without the given fact or knowledge of Christ could men ever have thought of the power of God in terms of the Babe lying

---

[1] I owe these illustrations to Miss Phyllis Dent.

in a manger, or pictured the love of God in terms of the Saviour on the Cross. Religious knowledge, that is to say, is not the same thing as religion. But religion is impossible without some religious knowledge. Teachers of religious subjects are well aware that it is possible for boys and girls in school to acquire considerable familiarity with the historical and documentary facts of religion and to pass examinations in scripture, yet for those boys and girls to be complete pagans because there is no *experience* in their own lives for such knowledge to interpret. To know *about* God is important for religion. But religion itself consists in *knowing* God. " This is life eternal, that they might know thee, the one true God, and Jesus Christ, whom thou hast sent."

Ideally, the practice of religion and growth in religious knowledge should proceed side by side. But whereas for an adult the approach to religion will be by way of knowledge and instruction *before* practice and worship, with children the reverse is true. The latter is, of course, the natural process. Man experiences first, and reflects upon his experience afterwards. A child, for example, is born into a family and experiences mother, father, brother William and sister Mary as living realities before he is able to understand the nature of the relationship existing between father, mother, sister and brother. The wise Christian parent will ask of his small child, not " What can I teach him about God ? " but " To what *experience* of God can I introduce him ? "

There is no doubt that the first religious experience possible for a tiny child is that of seeing his parents pray. If when the three-months-old baby is put to bed in his cot, father and mother kneel down beside him and say a simple prayer (Our Father, Grace, etc.), the infant will not, of course, understand the meaning of any words they use (and some part should be vocal), but he will catch something of the attitude and atmosphere of their action. As time goes on he will be more deeply caught up into it, and when he can talk he will want to join in and to ask questions about it. Then is the time for teaching and widening the child's conception of prayer.

Incidentally, a good deal of our failure as a Church in our dealings with children arises from the fact that they have been given in their homes no religious experience on which we can build. And we have frequently perpetuated the error by making worship and prayer follow teaching instead of preceding it. We have taught children in our Sunday schools *about* prayer and *about* worship and *about* the Church, in the hope that they would afterwards put these desirable things into practice. There is no need for surprise or disappointment that they do not, and in many cases cannot. Our first task is to enable them to *experience* prayer and worship, and to *experience* the fellowship of God's family, the Church, as living realities. Then, and only then, will the teaching about these things be significant. We make use of the same psychological process, as we shall see, when we are training adults in corporate and liturgical worship. The difference is that whereas for adults the *initial* experience is the presentation of the great facts of God's redemptive acts in Christ which are the fundamental presuppositions of all Christian worship, in the case of children we begin with the ' experience ' of prayer and the worshipful approach to God. That this difference of approach is a real and necessary one can easily be demonstrated by noticing the fundamental difference in the reactions of a child and an adult who are each taken to Christian worship for the first time. The child takes the services for granted. He does not question its validity or reality. He asks for information as to its meaning. " What mean ye by this service ? " " What is that thing for ? Why does he stand up ? " The adult reaction is quite different. If, as is almost certain, he finds himself out of his depth, he tends to question not the measure of his own ignorance, but the validity of the service. He proceeds on the assumption that what is not at once clear to him must be a bit odd and highly questionable. " What nonsense this all is ! I can't make head or tail of it." His first impulse is not to seek further information about it, but to dismiss it as stupid or incomprehensible. Hence the demand for simplified services that take nothing for granted. But such an attitude is the reverse of that required for worship. That is why we have maintained that for the vast majority of people in this country today, worship, or training in worship, must be preceded by instructions on the great fundamental truths of the Christian Faith. In other words, we need an *adult* catechumenate.

The case for adult education has been convincingly argued by Sir Richard Livingstone in his important book *The Future in Education*. He points out that while there are certain subjects that children can learn at school because they are practical—as *e.g.*, mathematics, chemistry, physics and languages—there are other and more vital subjects, such as history, literature, philosophy and religion, which can never have more than a minimum of significance for school-children, simply because of their inexperience of life. He says :

> " Let anyone consult his own experience. We have all probably learnt the Six Points of the Chartists at school. They were plastered on to our minds but never became part of the fabric, and, unless we have exceptional memories, the plaster has fallen off long ago. Was it ever worth applying ? What can children or adolescents *comprehend* of such things ? The day may come when they will have lived long enough in the world to perceive the meaning of politics, to have stood beside, perhaps to swim in, those obscure confused currents that sweep the world through political change. Then they

will understand. But that day has not dawned at the age of sixteen or even later." [1]

This is no less true of religion, and apart from all other considerations it is a strong argument in favour of some kind of adult catechumenate. Even in the case of those brought up in a Christian home and church, the habitual practices of prayer and worship must be filled out with ever-increasing significance, and the dogmatic background must be transformed into a working philosophy of life. As Sir Richard Livingstone says :

> " Habit without a settled principle is not enough. It may be enough perhaps in an age of settled belief; houses built on the sand are secure in fine weather. But ours is not such an age. The rains descend and the floods come and the winds blow and beat on us, and unless the foundations of character go down below the sands to a granite rock of principle, a definite philosophy of life, clearly seen and firmly held, the house is not likely to stand." [2]

II

It is not the purpose of this little book to attempt to devise a complete scheme for the application of the catechumenate to the particular circumstances and genius of the Church of England, but only to plead for a recognition of the necessity for some such development, and to suggest how such local ventures as are already being made in this direction may be extended and directed to the training of some of our fellow-countrymen in the almost lost art of corporate worship.

The worship of God is the true end for which man was

---

[1] Sir Richard Livingstone, *The Future in Education* (Cambridge U.P.), p. 26.　　　　　　　[2] Ibid., p. 122.

D

created.   But the word ' worship ' so defined means not only
the conscious worship of a congregation at special times and
in special places, but the whole dedication of human life to
the purpose of God.   It involves a recognition of the
sovereignty of God and the dependence of mankind upon
him, together with a recovery of the neglected truth of
vocation, secular as well as religious.   But the recovery of
this larger consciousness can only come about as and when
men return to an acceptance of the obligation to worship
God at the special times and in the special places set apart
for that purpose.   The general principle is built up from a
number of particular expressions of it.   The process cannot
be reversed.   Hence the importance of the recovery of the
primacy of worship in the life of the Church, and in her
approach to those who are at present outside her fellowship.
But since Christian worship is only possible when the basic
truths of the Christian Faith have been accepted, the Evangel
must precede the Eucharist, and some instruction in the faith
must come before the training in worship.

The first stage of any catechumenate will therefore be the
communication of the Christian dogma.   Vast numbers of
people in this country to-day simply do not know what the
Christian Gospel is.   Many of them would be highly
offended if you told them so.   They *think* they know already.
But to them the ' Good News ' of God's redemption of the
world through Jesus Christ, our Lord, who for us men, and
for our salvation, became Incarnate, is little more than the
Good Advice of a humanitarian kind, delivered by a gentle
Teacher who lived a long time ago, which is useful in personal
relationships, and might even be practised on a wider scale if
only men were different from what they are !   The first stage
of the catechumenate, therefore, will need to be something
like the sorting-rooms of a salvage collection depot, in which
the truth can be separated from the half-truth and the half-
truth distinguished from the wholly false.   It will need,

that is to say, to be a kind of discussion class in which people are encouraged to produce the ideas that they already have, so that when those ideas are false and inadequate, their holders can be shown where and why they are untenable and fall short of the Christian Faith. Many such discussion groups are taking place all over the country in all kinds of places and under many different conditions, ranging from the Padre's Hour in the Forces to the arguments 'that get round eventually to religion' among a group of fire-watchers or in the A.R.P. Post. Those of us who are responsible Christians should seize upon these opportunities, seeing them not as ends in themselves, but as the first steps in the development of what may come to be an organised catechumenate.

Quite recently I was invited to spend an evening with a group of young folk who had had several discussions on religion and had rather tied themselves into knots. So they said, " Look here, we're only going round in circles. Let's get someone along who is supposed to know something about it." In this particular case there was no opportunity of a follow-up, but at least by the end of a very intensive two hours some of the ideas put forward in all seriousness could be laughed at as absurd and inadequate, and most of the young people were enabled to realise that the Christian religion was something very different from what they had thought it to be, and very much more worthy of respect.

On another occasion I was invited to a certain house to meet some twenty-five young married men and women who wanted to ask questions about religion. The house was, in point of fact, a vicarage, but it was exactly similar in appearance to most of the other dwellings in the new and villa-type housing estate which formed the parish. The Vicar's wife had collected one or two young married women to discuss together the problems of bringing up children. The question of prayers and religion naturally cropped up, about which discussion was so lively that some of the women said, "Our husbands would be interested in this. Could we bring them along one evening?" They were duly brought, some of them perhaps with a little reluctance. But discussion soon became so heated and involved that it was decided to leave some of the questions for another evening, when I was invited to be present for the purpose of trying to deal with them. After the first half-hour an alert sounded, and all but three had to depart in haste to look after their families or to report to their posts. After twenty minutes the 'all-clear' was given, and every member returned. We had started at 8.15, but it was after 11 p.m. when we very reluctantly broke up, after a unanimous decision to meet again. The majority of these people were unattached to the Church. Many clergy are finding such experiences increasingly common.

Similar and more permanent groups are coming into being as a result of what is generally known as the 'Cell' movement. The basic conviction underlying the Cell movement is the need for a recovery by the Church of the sense of being the Body of Christ. Hence the term 'cell', the unit of life in the body. On the analogy of the disciples waiting in the upper room at Pentecost, a number of Christians come together for a time of corporate waiting upon God. Their purpose is to deepen their roots in God, and to put themselves into His hands. Their time together is spent partly in prayer and meditation, partly in discussion. It sometimes happens that one or two members of such a cell, conscious of their Christian responsibility to those who are 'outside', form another group among their friends and acquaintances for discussion. This second group is not a Christian Cell, because some of its members are not Christians. It is simply a group for the discussion and sorting out of ideas about religion, through which the Christian members try to get across to their friends what it is that the Church really believes and teaches about this matter and that.

In one town parish there was a small group of about seven men who, as the result of a Mission held in the parish, decided to meet together once a fortnight to ' chew things over '. After some while they decided that though they were all convinced Christians, they were doing nothing to propagate their faith. So they decided to turn themselves into a Cell and to ask God to show them some way of being useful as Apostles. After prayer and thought, they each agreed to tackle one or more of the non-Christian men among whom they worked on something of the following lines. " I say, Bill, you know that I'm a Churchman, and I know that you are not. Will you tell me, quite honestly, why it is that you don't go to church ? " The replies they collected from this investigation were then considered. To what extent was this criticism true, or that idea of religion false ? How far was this reply a real justification for not worshipping God, or that answer an indication that the speaker was just not prepared to bother ? In some cases the ' apostles ', finding that their workmates were either interested or labouring under completely false ideas, invited them to come to their gathering and thrash it out. " Bill, you remember me asking you why you did not go to church ? Well, there are a few chaps who come round to my house on a Tuesday night to talk these things over, and we've had some very interesting discussions. Would you care to drop in one night and have a yarn with us ? " Thus one or two newcomers appeared and the whole group went back to the beginning again, on the discussion level, going over old and elementary difficulties for the sake of the late starters. In some cases such groups have grown in the ' cellular ' fashion, each group dividing itself as soon as a certain number of members had been reached. In one parish there were eight or nine such groups, each having a leader or chairman. Each of these leaders formed another group, which met under the direction of the Vicar, so that the latter through them was reaching out to between fifty and sixty people.

An interesting and very fruitful venture along catechumenate lines was recently tried in a parish known to the writer. It was conceived by a men's Cell as part of the preparation for a Religion and Life Week, and was known locally as the 'Night Schools'. Seven or eight members of the Cell offered each to act as host for a weekly gathering in his house at which were to be invited various friends and neighbours, for the purpose of learning something about the Christian religion. Seven groups of people met therefore one evening a week for a period of eight weeks to listen to an instruction on the fundamentals of the Christian religion, given by one of the clergy, and followed by a time for questions and discussion. It says much for the success of the venture that whereas some ninety people in all were involved, many of whom were not otherwise attached to the Church, only one person dropped out during the whole of the two months.

Experiments of this kind are becoming increasingly common, and they point to a growing consciousness of the need for something analogous to a catechumenate. They are, in fact, attempts to meet that need. But they do not fill it completely, for however useful instruction and discussion groups may be in helping people to grasp the great basic truths of the Christian Faith, it is still a far cry from conscious and intelligent worship at a liturgical service. A catechumenate must at least embrace not only instruction in faith, but also training in worship.

Imagine a man who has taken part in a regular instruction and discussion class for some time, and who has become definitely interested, and perhaps partly convinced. What is the next step ? It may be that he will eventually evince a desire to be confirmed. But hardly yet. The Church and her worship are probably a closed book to him. What is likely to happen is that after the class or group one evening he will say to the Vicar something like this : " Well, Vicar, I must say it's all been very interesting, and I've learned a lot. I'll maybe come along to church one evening." The Vicar will probably smile and reply that he will be glad to see him there. But if that man does ' drop in ' to church one evening, the results may be disastrous, because he will find himself involved in a liturgical office which presupposes a far wider background of Christian culture than he has yet acquired, and which is drawn from a Prayer Book that he does not know his way about. It is likely that he will feel not only out of his depth, but what is worse, out of sympathy with the whole proceedings, and come rather sadly to the conclusion that religion is not quite so interesting in practice as it sounds in theory. What that Vicar ought to be able to say to the half-promise to " come along to church one night " is, " No, don't do that. You won't understand it if you do. Our Sunday worship is not really intended for fellows at your stage. But there is a little group of people which meets in church every other Tuesday evening who are trying to learn together something of the meaning and method of worship. Come along to that by all means. Then if later on you want to come to the ordinary services, you'll be able to join in properly."

In some parishes a small beginning in the development of a regular catechumenate might be made somewhat on the following lines. Instead of ' Evensong and Sermon ' at (say) 6.30 p.m., such people as desire enlightenment about the foundation truths of the Christian religion assemble. After a hymn (sung not as a religious exercise, but merely as a convenient means of getting people to join together in a corporate activity) and, perhaps, a brief act of recollection, there is a simple ' lecture ' on some basic element of Christian truth or life, followed by a short time for answering questions. Then the leader will conduct a period of ' guided silence ' (to be described later), in which he suggests a line of thought and allows sufficient time for the members of his audience to apply their minds to it in silence. The dominant ideas that have been suggested may then be summed up in one or two short prayers or collects, and another hymn is then sung. It is now 7 p.m. During the singing of this hymn such people as desire to leave may do so. Others may come in. Then follows Evensong pure and simple as an act of worship, for which the first half-hour has been instructional preparation. Mature Christians who have heard a sermon in the morning will probably welcome the opportunity to have Evensong without a sermon. If not, there is nothing to prevent them coming at 6.30 for the instruction. Those who are at the stage of being ' hearers ' only can thus attend the instruction without being involved in a liturgical service which they do not yet understand; until such time as they have had sufficient training (in the guided silences) in the art of corporate worship as will dispose them to attempt Evensong as such.

Provision might also be made for an occasional ' Question Night ', or even a Brains-Trust, and a periodic group discussion. It goes without saying that the parish priest must have a real grasp not only of that conversational style of presenting Christian dogma which is neither mission preaching nor lecture-room academics, but also of the technique of prayer and worship training, of which latter, more anon.

There is, however, one practical difficulty involved in the above suggestion that the address and discussion should be followed by or led into a time of guided silence of the kind to be described in the next chapter. If the leader is to safeguard the sincerity and integrity of the members of his group, he will not expect them to begin to pray in a manner which presupposes truths which they have not yet come to accept. But he cannot know in every case whether such truths as the group has considered have been accepted or not. Some may have done so, others not. Ideally, therefore, he ought to ask those who are not ready for a time of prayer to leave quietly. To do this, however, might cause embarrassment, and would necessitate the very thing he wants to avoid— viz., a break between the time of thinking *about* God and the act of turning *towards* him. This difficulty should therefore be explained to the people, and it should be made clear that though for the sake of quietness and courtesy all will stay for the prayer-time, only such people are asked to join in as feel that they can. The leader will also be careful occasionally to make this condition clear when he is leading the silence. "Let us, if we can, now commit ourselves to the Lord Christ." This provision will make for reality, and will enable the leader to link his teaching to an appropriate act of worship, or faith, or confession, or intercession at each meeting of the class or group. It is, of course, necessary to see that the subject-matter of the guided silence *does* arise from what has been taught, and does not take for granted truths which have not been considered. Teaching and worship training can procede *pari passu, but in that order*. In case of doubt, it is better to defer the introduction of the prayer and worship time than to run the risk of introducing it before the people are ready for it. The leader will be wise NOT to introduce it for the first few classes, until some groundwork has been covered. He will occupy the time with questions and discussion.

The kind of catechumenate beginnings here envisaged are for the most part small groups of people, meeting in private houses, vicarages, parish halls, youth clubs—wherever they can and whenever they can. In most cases they will meet on a week-night ; in some cases it may have to be on Sunday. There should always be opportunity for people to ask questions, and regular provision for open or group-discussion. When the group meets in a private room it may frequently happen that it will be more convenient, and also an aid to un-selfconsciousness, if people remain seated for the guided silences and worship-training in its initial stages. Sometimes—*e.g.*, for an act of praise—they may be asked to stand. The leader must be content not to take his group along faster than its average members can go. The questions and discussions will incidentally enable him to know how much they have grasped, and what are the particular mental muddles that most need sorting out. Frequently, the leader will have to digress very far from the outline syllabus he has in mind to deal with an issue upon which the group has seized. Flexibility and the readiness to go over the same ground several times in different ways are needed in this kind of work.

The following experience is one that must have been shared by many clergy in country areas during the last two or three years. The incumbent of a scattered rural parish used the opportunity provided by the black-out to take religion to the homes of his people by having cottage services instead of Evensong in church during the winter months. A cottage or farm-house at each of four strategic points was chosen, and each of the four was visited on Sunday evenings in rotation, so that every part of the parish was reached in the course of a month. The ' service ' consisted in a course of simple instructions on the meaning and structure of Evensong. After the talk the people joined together in that part of the service which had been studied, other prayers and Bible-readings being added from time to time. It was all very homely and informal, but people came to these services who had long since lapsed from church attendance. When Evensong was resumed in church, some of these lapsed folk came back—and stayed.

There are many clergy, too, who must have taken the opportunity presented by the broadcasting of Miss Dorothy Sayers' play cycle of *The Man Born to be King* to gather a little group of people in order to listen to it together. What an evangelistic opportunity !

In town parishes there might very well be given from time to time a series of public lectures on the Christian Faith, on the lines of the very successful course recently delivered by Dr. J. S. Whale at Cambridge. Not necessarily in the manner that would be appropriate to an academic audience, but a reasoned, dignified and clear-cut presentation of the fundamentals of Christian truth calculated to interest the best-educated and most intelligent members of local society. Such a series of lectures might very well be arranged once a year, perhaps in Lent. The lecturer should be someone from outside the town. If he, or she, is known to the general public through books or broadcasts, so much the better. It may very well be that as the result of such a course, one or two people are prepared to continue meeting for further discussion, and the beginnings of a catechumenate group may thus arise. The writer has discovered by experience that whereas to advertise a short ' mission ' in a parish usually attracts few if any folk who are not already members of the Church, a ' series of lectures ' does attract some. This is not due to any intellectual snobbery. Intellectual snobs are not usually disposed to consider the Christian faith at all ! It may, however, be taken as an indication that there are people ready to welcome what at least promises to be a reasoned and intelligent statement of what Christians believe, and why. One of the criticisms that may be made of the ' Religion and Life ' movement is that the speakers who function under this ægis sometimes come down more heavily on ' life ' than on ' religion '. For many churchpeople this is often a very necessary emphasis. There is a need to remind us that religion *has* something to do with housing, economics, work and wages. But to the outsider, ignorant of the theological presuppositions which the speakers at a

Religion and Life week have to take for granted, it is highly misleading, and he is liable to come away with the impression that the Christian Church exists for promoting economic security and social betterment.

Incidentally, if Religion and Life weeks are aimed at those outside the churches, their public meetings should not begin with prayer. *If* there is to be prayer (and it is by no means certain that there should be), it is far more suitable that it should come at the end, and that people who do not wish to remain for it may be given an opportunity to leave.

Another opportunity for clearing up some of the religious and theological muddles that clutter the minds of so many people in these days exists within the majority of societies and councils responsible for adult education. There is no inherent or diplomatic reason why the local W.E.A. or Adult Education Class sponsored by the L.E.A. should not include in its syllabus a course of lectures on religion. The only stipulation usually made is that the lecturer must be qualified, and must naturally make no attempt to proselytise.

The class attending such a course of lectures is *ex hypothesi* unable to become a catechumenate group, nor can it include prayer or worship-training. Its concern is religious knowledge rather than religion, and the lecturer must naturally respect his terms of reference. But it is a step in the right direction, and there may be some particular individuals who will desire to go farther once some of the common misunderstandings have been removed from their minds.

It may also be worth noting in passing that not only are most adult educational agencies ready to entertain lecturers on religious subjects (provided, of course, that there is sufficient demand among their students), but that they are also prepared to supply lecturers on a variety of subjects to church congregations. For the purposes of most boards of extra-mural studies, sponsored by the local or county education authorities, a church congregation, not below a certain numerical minimum, can rank as a society or club which can receive a lecturer supplied on the same terms as any other society. Not all clergy can keep abreast of, say, the condition of the Churches on the Continent, or be possessed of more than a smattering of economics. But it may be a very desirable part of the education of a congregation in matters very relevant to the implications of their faith (cf. Religion and Life) that they should from time to time be given information and instruction upon some of these larger issues. The Head of one well-known Board of Extra-Mural Studies often delivers a series of lectures of this kind in a parish church. Evensong is sung without a sermon, at the conclusion of which the lecturer, dressed in an academic gown, and standing on the chancel step, delivers his address.

ADDITIONAL NOTE ON THE PRESENTATION OF THE GOSPEL TO MODERN PEOPLE

Our plea that, since traditional Christian worship is so closely bound up with the Christian Creeds, those who have not accepted the Christian Creed should not be expected, or even encouraged, to take part in liturgical Christian worship may seem to some to be a counsel either of unattainable perfection or of despair. It would seem to be such a far cry from the semi-humanist, semi-materialist outlook of the average modern man to an acceptance of, say, the Apostles' Creed as to constitute almost an *impasse*. So let it be said that though we must not compromise about the fundamentals of faith which the creeds enshrine, we must at the same time be careful to present those truths not only in terms that modern people can understand, but also in relation to the kind of lives they have to live. Though there is, as has been said, a grave danger that in trying to make religion ' relevant ' to modern life, we dilute its content into a milk-and-water ethical idealism which neither St. Paul nor St. John would have recognised as the Christian Gospel; there is also a danger that we are so anxious to present the ' whole truth and nothing but the truth ' that we offer it as a theological system which does not seem to have anything to do with the problems which men and women are facing in modern society.   Though we must not leave them where they are, we must *begin* where they are.   It is the business of the Christian teacher and preacher to show that the Creed meets need.   This does not make it true, but it does make it worth consideration.   In the past we have been perhaps over-pragmatic.   We have laboured to show that ' Christianity works '.   The truth is, that in a non-Christian world it does not.   Witness the martyrs, ancient and modern.   As Bede Frost has said, the proper question to ask about religion is not " Does it work ? " (the question so frequently asked) but " Is it true ? "   Yet we must be careful lest in violent reaction against the pragmatic approach we fail to make contact with people *where they are*.   Our task, that is to say, is to show that the Creed is ' relevant ', while making clear that our reason for holding it is not primarily its relevance, but its truth.

It ought not to be difficult, in these days, to show that the Christian faith touches life at every point ; that it is, in fact, the ' answer ' (though not the short-cut solution) to human need in a way in which much that passes as ' Christianity ' is not.

Many men today are haunted by a sense of frustration and disillusionment.   They see the piling up on a vast scale of evil and tyranny that denies the sense of dignity and value which they have always believed to pertain to human life. They have a sense of *things gone wrong*.   They see themselves caught up in a vicious circle of having to do evil (*e.g.*, to kill and render homeless thousands of innocent German people) that good may come.   Some are becoming a bit doubtful of the good that is promised to come !   They perceive dimly that all our technical and scientific achievement, so far from saving us, has become the instrument of our self-destruction. If they don't see this, it is our duty to make them see it. They recognise dimly that " it's not the world that's wrong, but the people in it ". Here surely, written large over the face of Europe, is the truth contained in the Christian Doctrine of Original Sin. There is *something wrong with man himself*, which he cannot himself put right; but which God can put right, and has made available the way of salvation from it.

To those who look to some social or political scheme for salvation—*e.g.*, Communism—the truth of human sin applies equally. For it gives the lie to their optimism. There is no scheme or method of reorganisation which can cope with the basic fact of human selfishness. What could be more carefully devised than our present system of rationing, by which each has his exact share, no more and no less? Yet there is a black market. The Christian Gospel is good news about the very problem which lies behind all our personal, social and international problems—to wit, human self-centredness, or, as religion calls it, ' sin '. Christians to-day should be, not on the defensive, but on the offensive. Our creed does meet need. It is the only final and complete answer.

Do men feel helpless, seeing the things for which they have lived and worked destroyed before their eyes, unable to do anything to prevent it? Do they feel that they are cogs in a great impersonal machine of monopoly capitalisms and economic necessities (so called) which determine the pattern of their lives? Are they conscious of frustration; haunted by insecurity?

" Yes," says the Gospel. " Of course human life is wrong. Human nature is not as God originally made it. But this is still God's world. It is God, not man, who has the last word. Nor is God's purpose for human life confined to this short span of insecure and bewildering life. God has made man for fellowship with himself.   God is still God, whether men recognise the fact or not.   We are convinced about ' God the Father, Almighty, maker of heaven and earth '."

" Well," men say, " God may have made the world. Somebody must have done.   It can't have been an almighty accident.   But it does not look as if God were very much concerned about what goes on in it.   Why does not he do something about it ? "

" He *IS* concerned," says the Creed.   " He *HAS* done something about it.   He has come to earth.   For us men and for our salvation, he came down from heaven, was Incarnate by the Holy Ghost of the Virgin Mary, and was made Man.   And was crucified under Pontius Pilate. Whatever may be the suffering and travail of human life, he has shared it.   He does take responsibility for it."

" Yes," men say.   " But what good did it do ?   The world is no better.   Christ was put to death.   We're sorry about that, but it's no answer to our problems.   On the contrary, it makes it all worse.   It shows that the forces of evil in the world are stronger than the forces of good."

" But," says the Creed.   " Wait a bit.   That is not all. ' On the third day he rose again.'   However strong may be the forces of evil and destruction, they could not hold him."

" Granted.   But that was all a long time ago.   The fact that Christ rose from the dead then, does not help me *now*. It is a comforting thought.   But it's more than comforting thoughts we need.   We need power to conquer the evil forces now."

" Of course you do," replies the Creed.   " That is what I tell you.   ' I believe in the Holy Ghost and the Holy Catholic Church.'   Christ left behind him a body of men, filled with his power in a way that could be shared and transmitted.   Out of the human-nature-gone-wrong (which is your real problem) he has created a *new humanity*.   This new humanity is not self-centred (the old problem), but God-centred. It is not completely, of course, but it is in process of becoming so, and holds in trust the power by which all men, if they accept it on God's terms, may become so sufficiently to solve the problems that bother you."

Modern Man. " Well, if you mean that our hope is in the Church, then God help us ! Look at it. I ask you !"

The Creed. " Exactly, I thought you would say that. Now we shall have to get down to it. We shall have to do some Bible-study. We shall have, first of all, to distinguish the organisation of the Church from its real nature. You judge the Church by what you see. The most important part about it is what you don't see, and never can see from outside. You want Christ to-day. Well, you can't have him apart from the Church. Let me explain. . . . But quite apart from all this great mystery about the Church being the ' Body of Christ ', and having this great twofold function, first towards God, and secondly towards man and society, there is another thing. You told me that your son was killed in the Middle East. 'A valuable life cut short,' were your very words. Do you really believe that God's purpose for your boy—or for yourself, for that matter—can be defeated by a piece of shrapnel or an influenza germ ? I don't. ' I believe in the resurrection of the body (*i.e.*, of the whole, active, willing, personally identified life) and the Life Everlasting.' You may accept all that I tell you, or you may reject it. But if God be God, then at some time or other, in this life or the next, you'll have to come to terms with him. Granted all that you say about the frustration and evil of modern society, you still have your life, short and insecure though it be, to live. It is that for which you are personally responsible, however much conditions of life may invade and restrict your area of responsibility. For what you do with whatever is your area of choice you will have to answer for."

E

The business of the catechumenate-teaching (which is not quite the same as what used to be called ' mission-preaching ', the content being the same, but the context and technique different) is so to present the Christian Creed that men can realise that it has a very direct relation to themselves, and to the society in which they live. The Gospel *is* the Creed. The Creed *is* good news, and must be presented in such a way as to help men to see that it is. Further, they must be helped to see that nothing short of the authentic and orthodox Creed is either new or good. It must be made clear to them *why* brotherly love by itself is neither sufficient nor attainable; *why* the ethics popularly but inaccurately supposed to be contained in the Sermon on the Mount are inseparable from full Christian belief and life; *why* it is not enough to hold that Jesus Christ was merely the greatest of men; *why* faith is fundamental and what it is; *why* a good deal of the criticisms made about religion and the Church are irrelevant, since they do not exist for the purposes which so many people want religion and the Church to serve. All this groundwork must be covered before any idea of man's duty to worship God will have anything on which it can be fastened. Nor can all this teaching and sorting-out process be done properly unless there is some opportunity for people to ask questions, and to discuss freely their ideas and difficulties. Hence the practical advantage of the small group meeting in friendly and informal conditions. Hence, too, it should be added, the necessity of a leader who knows his theology and is possessed of endless patience.

It has been suggested [1] that the following words of Canon V. A. Demant might well be framed and hung up in every priest's study. They might well be taken as the ' standing orders ' of every Christian teacher, club-leader, cell-member, in fact, of every Christian who realises that as a member of the Body of Christ he has a duty of witness to fulfil :—

[1] By the Rev. A. G. Hebert in *Sunday Morning*, S.P.C.K., p. 139.

" Tell people only what they must do, and you will numb them into despair; you will turn the Gospel into a shaggy replica of the world's irreligious and nagging moralism, with its ocean-fulls of good advice. But tell them what they are, of their dignity as made in the image of God, and that their sins are wicked perversions of their nature . . . tell them that the world with its horrors is still God's world, though its true order is upside down; tell them that they can do all things through Christ, because in Him all the powers of their nature are directed and brought to fruition . . . and you will help to revive hope in this dispirited generation." [1]

[1] Quoted by the Rev. A. G. Hebert (*ibid.*), from *Christian Polity*, Faber & Faber, 1936, p. 39.

CHAPTER III

TRAINING IN WORSHIP

WORSHIP is man's response to God. The character of worship is therefore determined by the worshipper's conception of the nature of God. Christian worship is the response to God as he has made himself known through the history and genius of the Jewish people, through his Incarnation in Christ and through the Pentecostal gift of his Spirit upon the newly-formed Church. Christian worship, that is to say, arises from and depends on the truths enshrined in the Christian creeds. It presupposes the acceptance of two truths: first, that God is, and second, that God has revealed himself to and acted towards man in Jesus Christ, who, as Brunner puts it, is " God's own Word about himself ". All monotheistic worship involves the first of these two truths, but only Christian worship acknowledges that the Eternal, Creator of the universe, is he " who for us men, and for our salvation, came down from heaven, and was incarnate by the Holy Ghost of the Virgin Mary, and was made man ". That is why, as has already been said, those who do not accept this truth cannot, *ex hypothesi*, take part in Christian worship.

It does not lie within the scope of these pages to offer an apology for or an explanation of the centrality of worship in religion. Indeed, the word ' religion ' implies worship. ' Religion ', which comes from the same family of words as ' league ', ' ligament ', ' ligature ', means ' that which binds ', that which binds man to God. We are bound to God by the fact of our creatureliness; by the fact that he is God, and we are his people. " Be ye sure that the Lord he is God, it is he that hath made us and not we ourselves." It is the recognition of this fact that is the essence of religion and the mainspring of worship.[1]

Worship may, of course, take many forms, even within the Christian tradition. It may be sacramental or prophetic, simple or ornate, spoken or silent (as with Quakers), ordered or ' free '. The worship of the Anglican Church, following the main stream of Catholic tradition and practice, is of two kinds, sacramental and non-sacramental, and both are strictly ' liturgical ', and having what is commonly called a ' fixed form '. In view of the fact that certain Christian bodies, notably the Free Churches, regard such a fixed form as a hindrance rather than as an aid to worship, and that there are many others who regard prayers ' out of a book ' and ' constant repetition of the same thing ' as mechanical, it may be convenient, before going farther, to summarise the argument for ordered, as opposed to spontaneous, worship.

These arguments are of two kinds : (a) theological and (b) practical.

(a) Theological.

Christian worship was born in the worship of the Jewish synagogue. The first Christians, Peter, James, John and the rest, were Jews, nourished in the regular routine of synagogue worship every sabbath, and periodic pilgrimages to Jerusalem where they would take part in the sacrificial ceremonial of the Temple. It is significant that Our Lord himself went " as his custom was " to the synagogue on the sabbath day. Not, we may suppose, because he was in complete agreement with everything that was said and done there (on the contrary, he deliberately amended the Law of Moses and disputed with the Scribes and Pharisees), but because he accepted that worship as right in principle. It is true that he overturned the tables of the money-changers and cast out them that bought and sold in the Jerusalem

[1] Cp. The Athanasian Creed : " This is the Catholic Faith, that we worship . . ."

Temple. But he did not overthrow the altars and cast out the priests ; again, not because he regarded the Old Covenant and its derivative worship as adequate, but because what those priests and altars stood for was right in principle. The worship of the synagogue consisted of Scripture-readings, psalms, prayers and a sermon. That of the temple was a variety of ceremonial sacrifices. But both were highly liturgical, having a fixed form which assigned to ministers ,and congregation each their due and proper part. It was inevitable, therefore, that Christian worship, which in the lives of the first Christians only gradually became distinguished from its Jewish forerunner,[1] should contain much to which they were accustomed in the synagogue, and retain its characteristically liturgical form.

In the Old Testament a great deal of attention is given to the ordering of corporate and ceremonial worship, and great stress is laid on the need for correct performance and accuracy of detail. Moreover, though there was frequent need for the prophets to remind the people that the mere repetition of these forms was no adequate substitute for personal and social righteousness, there is no suggestion that such worship could be dispensed with, or that its character should be changed. Indeed, such visions of God and heaven as were vouchsafed to the Bible mystics always picture the worship of heaven as highly liturgical in character. To argue, therefore, that this is the way in which God wants to be worshipped is not so far-fetched as it might seem to some, when we consider the immense advantages that liturgical worship has over its alternatives.

(b) Practical.

1. *It is Truly Congregational.*—When people are praying their personal and individual prayers spontaneity and freedom are highly desirable qualities. But in corporate worship

---

[1] Except, of course, in the case of the Eucharist.

the individual is subordinate to the group. His function is not to follow his individual urges while his neighbours follow theirs. It is of the essence of corporate worship that all worship *together*—*i.e.*, join in the same act, follow the same theme, and for this purpose a procedure and subject-matter that are known beforehand are almost a necessity. In those traditions where the minister voices (often long) extempore prayers it is hardly possible for the congregation to be anything more than passive listeners. With the best will in the world they cannot pray and worship as actively as they ought, because by the time they have brought their thoughts to bear on one theme, the minister has passed on to something else. Where the framework is fixed and the words and acts well known, the members of the congregation are able to put each his own act of will and intention into the movement of the service. Moreover, it is of the essence of ordered liturgical worship that it assigns to priest and people each their proper part in the saying or singing of the service.

2. *It Safeguards Beauty and Dignity.*—The impulse to worship is the impulse to give to God the very best that we can offer. (Though the desire to come to church in our ' Sunday best ' can be debased into mere self-display, it is at bottom a very natural and right desire.) This will naturally express itself not only in beautifying the church building and its appointments, but will include the language by which our aspirations are expressed. It is no compliment to God to address him in thoughtless and slovenly speech, and it is a curiously illogical attitude which is careful about architecture and careless of articulation. It is surely natural that public worship should be composed of the best expressions of human aspiration that can be found, especially those which are drawn from the Bible and have been hallowed by centuries of reverent usage. We are especially fortunate in England in that the age which saw the translation of the Bible into English and the arrangement of our Prayer Book in its

present form was the age at which the English language was at its best. Moreover, experience shows that very few modern prayers wear as well as the ancient ones.

An age so incredibly vulgar that it can turn majestic themes of Mozart and Beethoven into Jazz dance tunes, and the air of the 'Hallelujah Chorus' into 'Yes, we have no bananas', is not likely to produce language adequate for the worship of God. It is significant that the Free Churches are coming more and more to follow a fixed form in their worship and are making considerable use of the Anglican Book of Common Prayer.

3. *It Secures Balance and Restraint*.—Christian ministers are no more free than most other people from the fascination of their own pet ideas. To leave the ordering of public worship to one man, be he priest or layman, is to run a grave risk of a disproportionate emphasis upon those aspects of Christian truth which appeal to the leader, to the neglect or even exclusion of those which do not. The Christian Faith is vast and many-sided. The Christian Calendar, with its regular round of feasts and fasts, and its careful attention to all the great truths of the Creeds, maintains a right balance, and delivers the congregation from ministerial idiosyncrasies and the limited understanding of any one mind.

The same right proportion of the various aspects of Christian worship—Adoration, Confession, Thanksgiving, Intercession and Petition—is also secured by the Prayer Book.

It is a further characteristic of traditional Christian worship that it is restrained.

> " Emotion glows in its depths, but it smoulders merely, like the fiery heart of a volcano, whose summit stands out clear and serene against the quiet sky. The liturgy *is* emotion, but it is emotion under the strictest control . . . If prayer is ultimately to be fruitful and

beneficial to a corporate body, it must be intense and profound, but at the same time normally tranquil in tone." [1]

While it provides expression for the deepest levels of devotion, it avoids rash and emotional utterance. Some of our popular hymns, unfortunately, avoid this wise principle. ' When I survey the wondrous cross ' is an exceedingly fine hymn, and contains a degree of consecration which ought to be true of all Christians. But the frequent and hearty mouthing of " Love so amazing, so divine, demands my life, my soul, my all ", while one puts twopence into the collection cannot but be weakening to the character. This may be an extreme example. But it will suffice to illustrate the wisdom of restraint in liturgical worship.

We shall not serve the interests of true religion by a departure from the liturgical worship of the Prayer-book. The tendency to substitute a monthly ' Young People's Service ' for Evensong; and gradually to alter the emphasis of the Divine Office by the inclusion of more and more ' modern ' prayers is a policy which is short-sighted and superficial. That there must be training in the art of worship, and that such training will involve experimentation and the use of many liturgical forms taken out of their liturgical setting is not questioned. But let such training be recognised for what it is: means to an end, and that end the intelligent use of those forms of sacramental and non-sacramental worship which within the providence of God have come to be the liturgical inheritance of the Anglican Church.

To the actual business of worship-training we will now turn. Worship is an art which can neither be acquired without practice nor taught without technique. It has already been said that it presupposes some grasp of the

[1] Romano Guardini, *Spirit of the Liturgy*, trans. by Ada Lane.

Christian doctrine of God, and a belief that he is an ever-present reality. "They that draw nigh unto God must believe that he is, and that he is a rewarder of them that diligently seek him." Hence, in practice, a period of worship-training will follow immediately upon some time spent in thinking about God. That is why it was suggested in the Sunday evening catechumenate that the guided silence should come *after* the address and/or discussion. The reason for this is clear. To say to people who are at the stage of being hearers only and who have just come in from a variety of occupations, about which some of them may still be thinking, " Let us recollect the presence of God," is to run a grave risk of creating mental vacuity. The great difficulty that so many people have in their attempts to pray and to worship is that God is so much less real to them than the immediate circumstances of their lives or of the war. Meals, work, newspapers, cinema, money are all part of their everyday lives. They are real, tangible, important. God is not to them real. He seems, on a superficial reckoning, to be so much less important than wages, or winning the war, and not only less immediately important, but vastly more nebulous and vague. They cannot think of him in the concrete way that they can think about their material environment. The purpose of the preliminary address or instruction, therefore, is not only to impart some piece of knowledge about God, but to assist the hearers to realise that he is real. Once their minds have been stimulated into thinking *about* God, it is not difficult to turn their minds *towards* God in a personal way. The first step in worship-training, therefore, is to help people to pass from thinking of God as *him* and to approach him as *thou*, and in order to make this crucial movement of mind and spirit, three conditions are required. The first is adequate *time*, the second is *silence* and the third is skilled and understanding *guidance*.

The English are not a rapid-thinking people, and for people of any race the pace of thought becomes slower as the field of thought becomes less familiar. However slick a man may be in arithmetical calculation, or in seizing the advantage in a business deal, however quick he may be in realising at what precise point a complicated piece of mechanism has broken down, he will find that his thought-processes in the things of God are very much slower and more hesitant until he has had considerable experience in prayer and worship. In any case, prayer and worship should never be hurried. The leader will, therefore, be careful to see that he allows sufficient time for his con-gregation to bring their minds to bear upon the various steps of aspiration through which he is leading them. The very fact that those who are unaccustomed to prayer and worship will take time to bring their thoughts into a Godward direction makes necessary a period of silence in which they may be able to formulate such thoughts as they can before they are expected to give those aspirations expression in words. Moreover, silence itself makes valuable suggestions of awe and reverence. " Be still, then, and know that I am God." The request that there should be more silence in our church services is one that comes frequently from young people. " It is obvious ", writes Miss Evelyn Underhill, " that . . . an ordered use of corporate silence, with all its advantages of freedom, sincerity, and inwardness, must enrich and deepen the worshipping life of the Church ; and should never have been allowed to fall into desuetude." [1]

But it must not, of course, be an *empty* silence. I once heard of a certain secondary school where it was the custom to have a time of prayer only one morning a week. When the school was assembled, the Headmaster and the staff filed in and took up their respective places on the platform. After the various notices and announcements, the Headmaster

[1] E. Underhill, *Worship*, p. 95.

reverently bowed his head and said, " Silent prayer ". The boys likewise bowed their heads, and there was silence. But one wonders whether there was any prayer. It is the leader's responsibility to stimulate the movement of mind, and to provide sufficient direction for the people to know what they are supposed to be doing in the silence, yet allowing each free to do it in his own best way. This is where skill on the part of the leader is needed.

Let us imagine that a parish priest has been taking his small group of ' hearers ' or catechumens through the Christian teaching about the Incarnation. He has made clear to them that the central truth of the Christian Faith is that the " One above " is the " One who came down ". He has further helped them to realise that the Christian life is a life the roots of which are " hid with Christ in God "; that it arises from the fact that Christ lives now, and is ever present to those who turn to him. Assuming that he is assured that those present have arrived at that point when they can begin to pray Christian prayer without insincerity (it may be necessary for him to give those who are not yet ready the opportunity to leave before the time of prayer begins), what are the first stages through which he will naturally try to lead them ? First, must clearly be that of recollection. He must give them some help in realising the reality and presence of our Lord, and sufficient silence in which to do it. He will make use very frequently of the language of Holy Scripture, partly because of its suggestive qualities, and partly because his ultimate purpose is to lead them to liturgical worship, which is highly scriptural in derivation and style. The second stage will be that of helping them to approach nearer to our Lord as individuals, possibly in an act of dedication, or asking for his grace and guidance, or maybe in making an act of thanksgiving for his Incarnation. Suppose the group has met in the evening, and the act to which the leader intends to direct the minds of its members is that of personal committal. He may proceed thus (being careful to maintain adequate pauses between each phrase or idea. For the sake of clarity * indicates a pause of approximately 3–5 seconds; * * = 6–10 seconds and so on):

"Abide with us, O Lord, for it is towards evening, and the day is far spent."

*

" When it was evening, came Jesus, the doors being shut, and said, ' Peace be unto you '."

*

" Thomas saith unto him, ' My Lord and my God '."

* *

(The leader may find it convenient and useful to summarise this introductory period with a short prayer.)

O Lord Christ, we believe that thou art here present, though with our human eyes we cannot see thee. Help us, each one, daily to know more of thee, to grow in thy strength and to live with thy life. This we ask for thy Name's sake.[1] Amen.

Now let us try, so far as we are able, to commit (offer or give) ourselves to him . . * . . all that we are . . * . . all that we hope to be and to do . . * * . . our homes . . * . . our work . . * . . our pleasures of mind and body . . * . . our hopes and our fears . . * . . and ask him that in all the circumstances of our daily lives we may come to find in him the Way, the Truth and the Life . . * . . that we may dwell in him and he in us.

* * *

[1] *Note.*—It may be thought that such a conventional termination is redundant. It is, however, essential to avoid all possible sources of distraction. People must not be left wondering whether they are expected to say ' Amen ' or not, and if so, when. The use of such an ending relieves their minds by making it obvious when and where ' Amen ' is to be said.

> Lord Jesus, Master Carpenter, who on the Cross,
> through wood and nails, didst furnish for man his
> whole salvation ; wield thou thy tools within our wills,
> that we, who come to thee rough-hewn, may by thy
> hand be fashioned to a truer beauty. This we ask, for
> thy Name's sake.[1] Amen.

Such an act as this will take no more than three minutes,
even if the leader is careful, as he should be, to say his part
slowly and deliberately. On the first and possibly second
occasions he may attempt no more than this. Later he may
follow on with a few biddings to intercession or thanksgiving,
conducted in a similar manner. (See pp. 75–77.) It is,
however, essential that whatever is to be the ' subject ', such
elementary beginnings in the art of praying together should
always start with an act of recollection. The leader will also
be wise to begin the ' response ' to that recollection with an
act of personal dedication, and to continue the practice until
his people have really grasped the fact that we must *come* to
our Lord before we can make our intercessions and thanksgivings and confessions. In the somewhat disproportionate
predominance that is given to intercession services at the
present time, there is a danger of leading people to suppose
that intercession is something that can be done apart from
their own personal dedication. This is not so. We cannot
send people to our Lord upon celestial trains of prayer. We
can only *bring* them. What matters in intercession is not the
recital of lists of names, but the will and intention offered by
those who intercede on behalf of those for whom they would
pray.

This matter of right approach is of quite vital importance.
The leader who hopes really to train his people in the art of
prayer and worship will be extremely careful never to plunge
them into any act of thanksgiving, confession, petition or

<hr>

[1] See Footnote on page 67.

intercession without a preparatory act of recollection and dedication. It may very well be that on the first two or three occasions the priest will not attempt to take his little group of beginners any farther than this first stage of recollection and dedication, as suggested above; but he will never omit it. The purpose of all prayer and worship is not (of the two alternatives) to make *us* more real to *God*, but to make *God* more real to *us*. It is not as if we should say, "O God, here we are. Please give us your attention for a few minutes, as there are one or two matters we want to put before you." In the first place, it is unnecessary to call God's attention to us. "And it shall come to pass that before they call, I will answer; and while they are yet speaking I will hear." Neither, secondly, is prayer a method by which we try to persuade God to do something that *we* want done. The purpose of prayer is to put ourselves into the way of doing what God wants. A recently published pamphlet issued for the guidance of members of a certain society contains the following piece of advice: "Bring God into the things of your everyday life". It is not mere quibbling to say that such advice is fundamentally misguided. It should run, "Bring the things of your everyday life to God". It is very natural that Christian apologists should strive to show that God is 'relevant' to modern life. But ultimately what man must do is to make modern life relevant to God.

"Whenever we try to use our religion as a solution of our temporal problems, caring more for that than for God and his glory, we fall under the same condemnation. I have heard speakers commend the cause of Christian Missions on the ground that to spread the Gospel, at any rate under Anglican forms, is a way of consolidating the British Empire; but short of that sort of vulgarity, we are all under the temptation to call in Christian faith as a means of delivering us from the agony of war, caring more for our own escape from that torture than for God's glory.   It is very natural; it is a state of mind with which we must all sympathise; but it is at best sub-Christian." [1]

The wise leader will, therefore, be careful to get the right emphasis from the very beginning, and thus help his people by example and frequent practice to realise that the essence of all prayer and worship is a lifting up of our hearts to God, and the dedication of our whole lives to him.

The choice of words and phrases will, of course, depend on the particular emphasis the leader wishes to make and the particular thought that he chooses as his theme.   In the example quoted above the theme chosen is clearly that of our Lord's presence.   If, however, the subject of the talk and discussion has been that of Christ's birth, then the guiding of the preparatory silence may run something like this:

Let us think in silence of this great truth that God himself has come to earth, and shared our human life, with all its joys and sorrows, weakness and pain; that he has not left us alone and in darkness, but that God has visited his people.

*

"And the angel said to Mary, ' Behold, thou shalt conceive in thy womb, and bring forth a son, and shall call his name Jesus '."

*

They all were looking for a King,
To slay their foes and raise them high,
He came, a tiny baby thing,
That made a woman cry.

*

[1] Wm. Temple, *Readings in St. John's Gospel*, pp. 83–84.

" The Word was made flesh and dwelt among us, and we beheld his glory."

*

" Behold the tabernacle of God is with men, and he will dwell with them, and they shall be his people."

*

Let us, then, in company with Mary and Joseph, with wise men and simple shepherds, worship him for what he is, true God and true man, King of kings and Lord of lords, the eternal Word of God made flesh.

* *

Let us enthrone him in our hearts, and offer to him our whole selves . . * . . that in our daily life . . at home . . * . . at work . . * . . in our love of our families and friends, we find in him our strength . . our joy . . and our peace . . * * . . that he for whom an inn could find no room may never again be crowded from our hearts.

* *

Let us pray :

Almighty God, who didst stoop to raise our fallen race by the child-bearing of Blessed Mary ; grant that we who have seen thy glory manifested in our manhood, and thy love perfected in our weakness, may daily be renewed in thine image, and conformed to the likeness of thy Son, Jesus Christ, Our Lord.[1] Amen.

Or, the Collect for Christmas Day would be equally suitable.

The most important part of this kind of guided-silence activity, is *what the people do with the silence*, and this will in turn depend on the extent to which their imaginations are fired, their emotions kindled and their wills moved by the

[1] This prayer is taken from *Cambridge Offices and Orisons* (Mowbrays).

instruction or address, and the actual language which is used to direct their aspirations in the silence. The leader will therefore be careful to chose such words and phrases as will appeal to the imagination, while conveying suggestions of the numinous, of a right mystery and awe. Both aspects are necessary. The phrase " Holy, Blessed and Adorable Trinity " fulfils the second condition, but for use with those on the threshold of Christian worship would not meet the first, because there is nothing in it on which the imagination can fasten. The phrases suggested above do, however, fulfil both conditions.

Further, since it is the silent activity that matters most, the leader will be careful in his control of the length of the silence. Experience makes one sensitive to the significance of a corporate silence. It may frequently be that the leader will be conscious that a particular period of silence is more significant than he anticipated that it would be. He may therefore prolong it a little. But at the first indication—a shuffle, or a fidget—that one or more members of the group have ' finished ', he will terminate it by passing on to the next thought.

At this point we must pause to distinguish the method of approach to the *content* of prayer and worship from the *technique* which is used to call forth and express it. The first steps in *content* are, as has been said, recollection and dedication. Later, dedication will be associated with the beginnings of praise and adoration. Thanksgiving, confession, intercession and petition will be introduced in their due order and proportion. But what *is* the due order? Theoretically and ideally the next stage after adoration should be confession. It is when man draws near to God that he becomes conscious of his own sin and unworthiness. Isaiah, on seeing the vision of God's majesty, exclaims, " Woe is me, for I am undone ; because I am a man of unclean lips, and I dwell in the midst of a people of unclean lips ; for mine eyes have seen the King, the Lord of Hosts ".[1] St. Peter cries, " Depart from me, for I am a sinful man, O Lord ". But it is extremely doubtful if such a response would come naturally from a generation like ours, to whom the reality of God is vague and dim, and the holiness of God almost non-existent. People to-day are not aware of sin *qua* sin, though they are conscious that things are not what they ought to be. Only after definite teaching will they be enabled to relate this sense of things having gone wrong to what in religion is called ' sin '. The stage at which such teaching is given will depend on the leader. That it ought to be given early is certain. For if man is not ' under the curse ' of sin, then salvation is unnecessary and irrelevant. All I am concerned to say at this point is that the leader will not introduce confession till he has taught his people something of the nature of sin. That he must do this at a very early stage in the proceedings is obvious. The aspects of prayer that come most naturally or impulsively from people to-day are those of petition and intercession. The leader will be wise to make use of this impulse, so long as he is careful to make such prayer noticeably subordinate and logically subsequent to recollection, dedication and the beginnings of praise.

The vital difference between the guided silence *method* of doing these things and that which consists merely in extempore or recited prayers, is that in the latter case the congregation tends to be one of merely passive listeners. By the former method they are invited and helped to *do* something with their mental and spiritual faculties. The leader's task is to call forth real activity of mind and spirit. Hence the advantage of the right use of silence.

But very soon there will be the need to provide some vocal means of expressing something of what has been done in the silence. Here the ' say-after-me ' prayer or collect has its uses, provided that it is expressive of thoughts that people

[1] Isaiah vi. 5.

have been given time to think beforehand, and not just switched on for unpremeditated and parrot-like repetition. A much more useful and appropriate device, however, is the use of the versicle and response, and what for our present purpose may be regarded as an elaboration of the versicle and response, the litany. The fact that this device is so ancient (it was taken over into Christian worship from the synagogue services) is almost certainly due to its obvious practical advantages as a means of corporate expression.

> "The litany, or series of brief acts of prayer and praise with a fixed response, is, according to Heiler, one of the most archaic forms of common worship, and is still found in many tribal rituals. It is a simple and obvious device for securing the attention and united religious action of a group without service-books or ritual knowledge; for all the congregation needs to know is the choral response by which it endorses the leader's prayer." [1]

Incorporated into the guided-silence technique it not merely serves to " endorse the leader's prayer ", but to give vocal expression to the prayers which under his direction each worshipper has made. It has the further merit of being the first beginnings of liturgical worship. The next step in *method*, therefore, will be the introduction of the litany-form, consisting of bidding—silence—versicle—response. The point of interspersing a versicle between the bidding and the response is that it enables the leader to control the length of the brief silence, and frees the minds of his people from the otherwise inevitable distraction of wondering when to say the response, as would most certainly be the case if he merely said, "After each bidding, there will be a short silence before we say the response." He will say, rather, " We will express our prayers corporately in the

[1] E. Underhill, *Worship*, p. 100.

words ' We praise thee, O God ', after I say the words
' Through Jesus Christ, our Lord '. This device, though
quite common in use, seems in practice to be almost
invariably limited to the versicle and response :

> Lord, hear our prayer,
> And let our cry come unto thee,

which, though of Prayer-book origin, is not suitable for all
the occasions on which it is made to do duty, and suffers
from the defect of suggesting a rather distant, if not absentee,
God. Holy Scripture and the Prayer-book provide abundant
material for an almost endless variety of such versicles and
responses. A classified selection, drawn from the psalter, is
given at the end of this book.

There is a good deal to be said for making such a response
into an act of faith, and prefacing it with some scriptural
statement of trust in God. For instance, the kind of general
intercessions that are common during a time of war might be
conducted somewhat as follows : (It is here assumed that the
acts of recollection and dedication have been completed.)

Leader. Let us commit to God the people of this
nation, and pray that we may be kept from pride and
harsh judgments . . * . . from all desire for revenge
. . * . . and from false reliance upon our own strength.

* *

" They that wait upon the Lord shall renew their
strength."

*

Lord, we believe.
People. *Help thou our unbelief*.
Leader. Let us pray for those who carry the heavy
responsibility of leadership at this time, that they may

act always from the right motives, and with a high sense of their duty to God, the Father of all.

* *

" If any man lack wisdom, let him ask of God, who giveth to all men liberally, and upbraideth not."

*

Lord, we believe.
People. Help thou our unbelief.
Leader. Let us commit to the care and keeping of God all those who are separated from their homes and families by the circumstances of war . . * . . those who are serving in the armed forces . . * . . especially those whom we know and love . . * . . and pray that they may be kept ever close to the things which belong to men's peace.

* *

" Thou shalt keep him in perfect peace whose mind is stayed on thee."

*

Lord, we believe.
People. Help thou our unbelief.
Leader. Let us remember all who suffer . . . in battle and air-raid . . * . . in bereavement . . * . . in captivity and persecution . . * . . all who wait in anxiety for news of their loved ones . . . .

* *

" I know that neither life nor death, nor angels nor principalities nor powers, nor any other creature shall be able to separate us from the love of God which is in Christ Jesus, our Lord."

*

Lord, we believe.
People. Help thou our unbelief.
Leader. And let us not forget that, as Christians,

we are bound to pray for our enemies. Let us pray, therefore, for those who fight against us, that they may return to the way of righteousness and peace . . * . . that we and they may learn to live together as God's children.

* *

" God so loved the world that he gave his only-begotten Son, that whosoever believeth on him should not perish, but have everlasting life."

*

Lord, we believe.

People. Help thou our unbelief.

Leader. Let us commit the future to God, and pray that he will dispose the issues of this present conflict that they further his good purpose.

* *

" The Lord is King, be the earth never so unquiet."

*

Lord, we believe.

People. Help thou our unbelief.

Leader. Lastly, let us commit to our Lord this whole suffering world, and pray that he will sanctify it with his own Passion, and bring out of this present agony a regenerated mankind . . * * . .

Jesus said, " I, if I be lifted up from the earth, will draw all men unto me."

*

Lord, we believe.

People. Help thou our unbelief.

Leader. Let us gather up all our thoughts and prayers in the words which our Lord taught us, saying . . Our Father, which art, etc.

Note.—The use of such terms as ' sanctify ', ' regenerated ' is deliberate. Words like ' glorify ', ' sanctify ', ' hallow ',

' redeem ', have no exact synonyms, and they are authentic Christian terminology. They should therefore gradually be introduced in contexts where their meaning is unmistakable, so as to familiarise the worshippers with great Christian language.

All the various aspects of prayer and worship, praise, confession, thanksgiving, intercession and petition can be led in this way, and in the hands of a sympathetic leader the method can provide real training in corporate worship. The third step in *method* is to link the guided-silence scheme described above with some of the great acts of liturgical worship. Liturgical worship is primarily *expressive of an experience*. Though it has its suggestive side, reminding us of what we *ought* to think and feel, its chief function is to give vocal or ceremonial expression to what the worshipper believes, desires and feels. That is why people who are on the threshold of religion are almost bound to find the Church's liturgical services ' beyond them '. Liturgical worship only becomes possible when the worshipper has at least some of the experience that the liturgical form expresses.

Now, the purpose of the guided-silence method is to lead people into the beginnings of worshipful experience. It is therefore the prelude to the use of fuller liturgical forms. For instance, appropriate collects can, with great effect, gradually be introduced into the scheme outlined above, because they sum up or ' collect ' together all that the congregation has been thinking about for the last so many minutes. Very soon the conductor will, at his discretion, lead these times of guided silence, versicle and response into one of the corporate acts drawn from the Prayer-book as, for instance, the General Thanksgiving, the Prayer for all conditions of men, the Sursum Corda and others, which the congregation will say together with him.

To take a simple example of this approach. Suppose the

leader of a catechumenate group desires to introduce his
'hearers' to the use of the General Thanksgiving. He will
not begin by asking them to turn it up in the Prayer-book and
examine it, pointing out how right it is that we should thank
God for creation, Incarnation and all the blessings of this life,
and explaining 'unfeignedly' and 'the hope of glory' in
passing. The form of words is the terminus *ad quem*, not
the locus *ab quo*. He will begin, however, with a consideration of the truths relative to thanksgiving, and dependence
upon God. Then, using the guided-silence, versicle and
response method, he will arrange the subject-matter of his
biddings to thanksgiving in approximately the same order as
that in the General Thanksgiving. He may do this on
several occasions, until he feels that his people are thoroughly
familiar with the *experience* of thanking God for these things.
Then, and not till then, he will introduce the words of the
General Thanksgiving, *by which time those words will be
significant of an experience that is already theirs*. Except in
the case of those who have been categorised as A1 (the
faithful and intelligent Christians), the difference between
the use of such a liturgical form—*e.g.*, the General Confession
—*after* some time of guided and silent reflection, and merely
plunging straight into it without any such preparation, is the
difference between reality and unreality. Below are two
examples of this method, one illustrating an introduction to
the General Thanksgiving, and the other the Prayer for all
conditions of men.

It is assumed in both cases that the people have reached
the stage of accepting the relevant truths—*i.e.*, that of our
dependence upon God, of the Incarnation and redeeming
death of our Lord and the sacraments of the Church; in the
second case, the doctrine of the Church Catholic as the
Spirit-bearing Body of Christ.

THE GENERAL THANKSGIVING

Versicle and Response (announced beforehand).

V.   O praise the Lord with me.
R.   *And let us magnify his Name together.*

Or any one of those in the Appendix.

Leader. Let us give thanks to God . . for all that he is . . * . . for all that he has done, for us men and for our salvation . . * . . For the world that he has made . . * . . for the gifts of life and love . . * . . For the knowledge that he is our God, and that we are his people . . * * . .

" Be ye sure that the Lord, he is God, it is he that made us and not we ourselves.   We are his people." . . * . .

* *

O praise the Lord with me.
People.   And let us magnify his Name together.
Leader. For the beauty of the common things of earth, the splendour of the sea.   For the joys and inspiration that come to us through the world of nature . . * . . especially (here some local beauty spot or favourite place of recreation may be mentioned).

*

" The heavens declare the glory of God, the firmament sheweth his handiwork."

* *

O praise the Lord with me.
People.   And let us magnify his Name together.
Leader. For the constancy of God's gifts in nature, . . * . . for all those on whose skill and labour we depend for life . . * . . for the ministries of art, music and medicine . . * . . for the love of friends and family . . * . . for the privilege of work and worship.

*

" O Lord, how manifold are thy works, in wisdom
hast thou made them all.   The earth is full of thy
riches."

* *

O praise the Lord with me.
People.   And let us magnify his Name together.
Leader.   Most of all, let us thank God for his living
word and saving act in Christ Jesus our Lord, by whose
life and death and resurrection our redemption has been
wrought . . * * . .
" While we were yet sinners Christ died for us."

* *

O praise the Lord with me.
People.   And let us magnify his Name together.
Leader.   For the gift of the Church which is his
Body . . * . . for the sacraments by which his grace
is bestowed upon us . . * . . for the knowledge that
in him we have everlasting life.

* *

Jesus said, " I am come that they might have life . . .
more abundantly ".
O praise the Lord with me.
People.   And let us magnify his Name together.

There may follow a bidding for silence in which each may
add his own special and personal thanksgivings.   Then an
appropriate verse from scripture, and the versicle and
response.   All this will finally be led into the General
Thanksgiving *when the people are ready for it.*

THE PRAYER FOR ALL CONDITIONS OF MEN

Versicle and response (to be announced at the beginning).

V.   O Lord, show thy mercy upon us. ⎫ Or any others
R.   *And grant us thy salvation.*   ⎬ appropriate.

Note.—Though similar biddings to those on pp. 75–77 might naturally be used here, others are suggested below to avoid duplication.

The act of faith, drawn from Scripture, inserted between the bidding and the versicle is not always needed.   But its use is a wise general practice.

Leader.   Let us commit to God this our family, and all those among whom we live and work, and pray that we may learn to live together as his children . . * . . Let us pray, too, for the whole family of mankind, that the nations may so learn to love and serve God, the Father of all, that men may dwell in unity, peace and concord . . * *

" For the Kingdom is the Lord's, and he is the Governor among the people."

* *

O Lord, show thy mercy upon us.
People.   And grant us thy salvation.
Leader.   Let us therefore pray for all who are seeking to spread Christ's truth among the nations . . * . . for the Church, which is his Body . . * . . for the Church in this parish and country . . * . . For the persecuted Church of Germany, and the countries under her power . . * . .

For the Church of Russia . . * . .

For the Churches of India, Africa, China and the Americas . . * . . That the Church in all the world may be faithful to her Lord, and may be to all men the minister of his power and peace . . * * . .

Jesus said, " I will build my Church and the gates of hell shall not prevail against it . . * * . ."

O Lord, show thy mercy upon us.

People. And grant us thy salvation.

Leader. Let us pray that all who profess and call themselves Christians may be led into the way of truth, and hold fast to the faith, so that when, in his own time, our Lord shall gather us together into one fold, we may know the unity of the Spirit, in the bond of peace. * *

Jesus said, "And other sheep I have which are not of this fold, them also I must bring and there shall be one flock, and one Shepherd."

O Lord, show thy mercy upon us.

People. And grant us thy salvation.

Leader. Let us commit to our Lord all who suffer in mind or body . . * . . the bereaved and sorrowful; the lonely and unloved . . * . . all who lie on beds of pain . . * (especially . . .) all whose labour is without hope, without honour, without interest . . * . . for those who have no work to do . . * * . .

Jesus said, " Come unto me, all ye that labour . . and I will refresh you " * *

O Lord, show thy mercy upon us.

People. And grant us thy salvation.

Leader. Let us gather up all our thoughts and prayers by praying together the Prayer for all sorts and conditions of men, saying : " O God, the Creator and Preserver of all mankind . . . etc."

Herein lies the key to effective training in corporate and liturgical worship. The method outlined in the foregoing pages is based on the fundamental principle that liturgical worship is the goal, not the beginning, or even the text-book, of initiation into the Christian Church. Few will question the psychological soundness of this principle. It is axiomatic in teaching, that the way to teach certain kinds of truth is to enable the pupil to follow the steps by which truths were first discovered by men. For example, in the teaching of Christian doctrine the wise teacher will try to get behind the words which express a particular truth to the living experience that those words enshrine ;[1] probably suggesting that his pupils should try to put that experience into their own words, and then compare their formula with that which the Church accepts as adequate and authoritative. So in training in worship the same steps are followed. We begin with the great facts of Incarnation, the Cross, the Resurrection, by which God has revealed himself in the experience of mankind, and help our ' hearers ' to realise the living reality of these great truths, and their relevance to modern life and present-day issues. The second stage consists in helping our learners to turn these truths into their own thoughts and words in silent prayer, and supplying them for corporate expression with words by which the Church through many generations has expressed those same truths and aspirations. Finally, we can lead them into the full liturgical expression of those truths, now a part, and, we trust, a real part, of their own experience. When all this has been done, our catechumen can ' come to church ' and find himself ' at home '. He will find himself hearing, saying and singing words that are already full of significance. That which would have ' left him cold ' had it been his first introduction to Christian worship, is now warm with personal and experiential associations. He finds himself with a body of people speaking a language with which he is becoming increasingly familiar. He experiences the pleasurable thrill of one now able to express himself and understand a fresh language ;

[1] For an exposition of this see *Teaching Doctrine*, P. Dent (Nat. Soc.).

the sense of exhilaration of one who is in the first stages of appreciating great art or great music. He begins to wonder how he could have been so dull and impercipient as not to have realised its significance earlier.

But before this stage is reached a very important question has to be faced. To what service or services is our catechumen to be introduced? Is it to be Mattins, Evensong or Holy Communion? From the point of view of significance and familiarity, it does not much matter. If he has passed through the kind of training-stage we envisage, he will not only have been taught the Christian Faith, but he will have been introduced *experientially* (through the Versicles and Responses) to the language of the Psalms, and will have been led to a conscious and significant use of such liturgical forms as the General Confession and Thanksgiving, the *Sursum Corda*, the *Gloria*, the Grace, the *Sanctus*, and many of the Prayer Book collects. He will also have been introduced, in their appropriate context, to the Gospel Canticles, the *Magnificat*, the *Nunc Dimittis* and the *Benedictus*. He will be, under wise leadership, already familiar with parts of the *Te Deum*. At whatever service of worship he now finds himself, he will be on familiar ground. But it is nevertheless a very important matter of practical and doctrinal principle to decide not merely which is to be the first service to which he is introduced, but which is to be represented as that of primary obligation. To this question we must now turn.

CHAPTER IV

THE EUCHARIST

THE answer to the question, ' To what service should the catechumen first be introduced ? ' will not *of necessity* be identical with that to the question, ' What is the service of primary obligation ? ' The first question is one of technique, and must therefore be to a certain extent a matter of opinion. It will be decided by practical, local and psychological considerations. But the second is one of principle to which personal opinions are not, or should not be, relevant. This book is largely about technique. It is not our purpose to discuss doctrine, except in so far as it determines our technique. It is therefore outside our present scope to attempt to deal at all fully with the theology of Eucharistic worship, or to repeat much that has recently been written about the Parish Communion. But since the ways and methods of achieving an end must always be made subordinate to the end in view, a word about the objective of all our catechumenate work must be said.

Without question, the ultimate purpose of our work with any particular ' hearer ' must be his conversion and his initiation into conscious membership of and life in the Body of Christ. At the heart of this life is the Sacrament of the Lord's Supper. All down the centuries the mainstream of the Church's life has rightly been centred round the Gospel Sacrament. Described by a variety of names, each of which emphasises a particular and legitimate aspect of its truth and mystery, adorned and beautified by art and music, the Liturgy proper is the fulfilment of our Lord's command " Do this in remembrance of me ". The divine command alone is sufficient to put the primacy of this obligation beyond question and dispute. The Book of Common Prayer clearly assumes that Holy Communion shall be regarded as the primary obligation of Sunday worship. The Sunday sermon is to be preached after the Creed, where also the notices are to be given out. Though " there was never anything by the wit of man so well devised, or so sure established, which in continuance of time hath not been corrupted ",[1] the only logical conclusion that can be drawn from such directions is that the Book of Common Prayer assumes that full Church members will be present at the Lord's Table every Sunday and Holy Day. This is the Church's Family Meal. The Divine Offices, Morning and Evening Prayer, are the Church's family and daily prayers, based on the principle of the monthly recitation of the Psalter and the regular reading of Holy Scripture. That the Divine Offices became a popular Sunday devotion, as the vernacular names Mattins and Evensong testify, did not and does not alter the fact that they were never intended to be regarded as a substitute for the fulfilment of the primary obligation. They are the framework of the Liturgy proper. Mattins and Litany are preparation before, Evensong the Thanksgiving after, the " Lord's own Service on the Lord's own day ". It is sometimes argued that Mattins and Evensong, being in origin monastic offices, are unsuitable for the laity. Even if this were true, it does not alter the fact that the Prayer-book intends them for ordinary folk, as well as for the clergy, on whom they are obligatory. This intention may have failed to achieve practical fulfilment because of many other demands on the time of the laity. There are few, even among the most faithful, who are free to come to daily Mattins and Evensong. But the principle holds. They are by origin and intention *daily* offices or services. On Sundays and Holy Days primacy of place is

---

[1] *Concerning the Service of the Church.*

G

given to Holy Communion, a fact emphasised by the provision of special Collects, Gospels and Epistles.[1]

The goal and end of our work, therefore, is (for our immediate purpose) communicant life. There are not two kinds of Christians in the Church of England, communicants and others. Convention may recognise the latter, the Prayer Book does not, and in this it expresses the mind of the undivided Church, and the great and permanent tradition of Christendom.

Eucharist worship, then, being the end, at what point should our ' hearers ' be introduced to it ? Should their first introduction be to Holy Communion, or to Mattins or Evensong ? To a certain extent this will depend on the ' hearer ', the priest and the parish. There are, however, two considerations, which, though not matters of doctrinal principle, have a direct bearing on the question, and point to a particular answer.

Though the Sacrament of Holy Communion is rooted in mystery—the mystery of our Lord's Incarnation, Passion, Redemption, and the mystery of his Sacramental Presence—the fact that it is in essence an *action* gives it an essential simplicity which the synagogue-type of worship cannot by its nature possess. The Gospel Sacrament is to this extent easier to grasp (not ' understand ') than the less mysterious offices of Mattins and Evensong. There is an " outward and visible sign " the significance of which is unmistakable, even to the mind of a child. I can remember being aware of this at a very early age. When I was seven or eight years old I used to go to church with my father. After Mattins

[1] This is not intended to suggest that the daily celebration is out of accord with Prayer-Book tradition. On the contrary specific provision is made for it by the Rubric (at the end of *The Order of how the rest of Holy Scripture is appointed to be Read*) which runs :

" Note also, that the Collect, Epistle and Gospel appointed for the Sunday shall serve all the week after, where it is not in this book otherwise ordered."

followed a celebration, to which some, of whom my father was one, remained. It was a plain, north-end celebration, with the very minimum of movement, and devoid of any symbolic action. But when the people went up to the altar-rail and knelt down, and I saw the vicar administering the consecrated elements, I knew that the people had gone up to receive 'heavenly food'. This had never been explained to me. The central meaning of the rite spoke for itself, and had I been even younger I could not possibly have missed its significance. I realised, too, that here was a privilege I hoped one day to share. The Sacrament of Holy Communion is concrete, objective, dramatic. It is rooted in the Person of our Lord. It is the great proclamation of his Passion. "As often as ye do eat this bread and drink this cup, ye do shew forth the Lord's death till he come." This fact would seem to point to the wisdom of introducing the 'hearer' to the Eucharist before he is made familiar with the Choir offices.

A further fact seems to point to the same conclusion. In these days of theological and religious confusion, when there is so much popular misunderstanding about the nature of the Christian religion, as distinct from the vaguely humanist ethics, divorced from dogma, that so frequently passes for Christianity, it is the Church's obvious duty and wisdom to recover the supernatural Gospel of Redemption and all that is implicit in it. She must make it perfectly clear that she does not exist simply to be a society for the promotion of good causes, or to purvey moral uplift, but for the proclamation of revealed truth and the preservation of supernatural life. She must therefore be at pains to emphasise all that is distinctively *Christian*—i.e., 'belonging to Christ'. Good conduct and moral behaviour apart from faith in God do not belong to Christ. They may even hold a man back from him. The man-in-the-street says, "I can be as good as those who do go to church" (there are many who say this in a tone of voice that suggests that in point of fact they are very much better !). The Church's answer should be, " That may be so. It all depends on what you mean by ' good '. But, in any case, it is not the point. We do not exist to make men ' good ' as society judges goodness, but to make them *Christian*; to make their ' goodness ' God-centred, and not self-centred. We exist to make known the eternal truth of God, who for us men and for our salvation came down from heaven, and was crucified on a cross to save us from sin. We exist to bring men into the new humanity that Christ has created. We exist to worship God, and to share his sacramental life, not because we think that thereby the world will be a more congenial place to live in, but because he has commanded us ' Do this in remembrance of me '. As a matter of strategy, quite apart from theology, the Chuch should, in the present situation, stress all that is distinctively Christian in worship, teaching and living. The Sacrament of the Lord's Supper is the distinctively *Christian* rite.

There is therefore a strong case for making the Eucharist the first step of the ' hearer's ' initiation into the Church's worship. It may very well be that he may wish also to come to one of the Choir offices, and if he does, his catechumenate training will have already familiarised him sufficiently with the various elements of those offices to enable him to take an intelligent and worshipful part in them. But his first training in the worship of the service as a whole will be in the Liturgy proper. It is quite likely that our ' hearer ' has not been confirmed. But now, having been helped to realise that to be a Christian involves full membership in the worshipping community, he expresses his desire for full membership. At that point his Confirmation preparation (as distinct from his catechumenate training) begins. There may be others who have been confirmed but who have never made a proper start on their communicant life. These, too,

will be invited to attend the Confirmation preparation, the
emphasis of which should be not on Christian doctrine, but
on Christian living.   Here will be considered not only the
discipline and obligations of the new life in Christ, but also
there will be training in Eucharistic worship as such.   When
a man decides that he wishes to be confirmed, and while his
preparation is in progress, there should be laid upon him as a
definite obligation, and as part of his preparation, weekly
attendance at Holy Communion.   Where a 9 or 9.30 Parish
Communion is established, this will be facilitated, and his
presence will seem perfectly natural, for this *is* the parish,
family-worship.   But if the only celebration is at 8 a.m.
the principle holds.

TRAINING IN EUCHARISTIC WORSHIP

Training in Eucharistic worship must be distinguished
from the teaching of Eucharistic doctrine.   The two must
inevitably overlap, since the devotion derives from the
doctrine, but, generally speaking, the doctrinal teaching will
be largely a matter of class-work, whereas the worship-
training will be centred upon the actual celebration in
church.   The main aspects of Eucharistic doctrine will be
taught before the real training in Eucharistic worship begins.
The latter will differ in detail, though not in substance,
according to the custom of the parish.   Clearly, in parishes
where the holy mysteries are celebrated with traditional
ceremonial the worship-training will be facilitated, and will
be somewhat fuller in content than in churches where the
tradition is otherwise.   But the main purpose of the worship-
training will always be to enable the worshipper to enter into
the logic and *movement*, as well as into the devotion, of the
Liturgy.   So often to the uninitiated a liturgical service
seems to be a merely fortuitous assembly of prayers, readings
and hymns, and he is unaware of the devotional and liturgical

movement from the beginning to the climax. Especially is this true in the case of Mattins and Evensong. With the Communion Office the difficulty is less acute, since it is in essence a drama—*i.e.*, something done ; it has an obvious climax and some equally obvious elements of preparation. But to realise the significance of certain unmistakable points in the service is not enough. The purpose of training is to help the worshipper to see everything as an integral part of the Liturgy, and to follow each step in its logic from beginning to end. The admonition of Pope Pius X that communicants should learn ": not to pray at Mass, but to pray the Mass " applies as much to Anglicans as to Romans.

Some teaching about the sacramental principle, the Institution of the Sacrament of Holy Communion and its meaning, together with an outline of the structure of the Liturgy, will best be given in class. This knowledge can then be used as the basis for worship-training. There are various ways in which the relation of the doctrine to the structure of the Liturgy may be approached. The writer's own method is to begin with the three-fold action of our Lord at the Last Supper, and to show how this three-fold action is the basis of the Prayer-Book Service of Holy Communion, as of all other Liturgies. Thus :

1. He *took* . . . bread and wine. The *Offertory* and its meaning.
2. He *blessed* them.   The *Consecration*.
3. He *gave* . . . to his disciples. The *Communion*.

The Communion Office is analysed on a blackboard, and shown to consist of these three elements or acts, together with a preparation at the beginning and a thanksgiving at the end. The doctrine and the devotion are thus shown to be closely bound up together. Next it is explained that this structure is in essence that which has always been used from the earliest days of the Church. The relevant passage from Justin Martyr's *First Apology* (Vol. II of T. & T. Clark's 'Ante-Nicene Library', p. 64) is then read aloud and its description of the Eucharist related to the blackboard analysis of the Prayer-Book service.[1] Incidentally, the circumstances which gave rise to the writing of this Apology can be made a thrilling story for young people, and provide an excellent illustration of the ageless nature of the Gospel Sacrament and its centrality in the life of the Church. (It goes without saying that the Apology will not be used without some explanation of its origin.)

All this is more easily done in class and before the actual worship-training in church. In most cases those receiving instruction will be present at the Eucharist on Sundays, and will thus be able to relate the instruction to their worship. But it will be of great value to most of them to be helped to enter into the movement of the Liturgy at an actual celebration or series of celebrations.

The method of having a conductor in the nave who explains to the congregation the actions of the celebrant at the altar is too well known to require description. Given a good conductor, it can be a very effective method. But, especially where an incumbent is single-handed, it is not always possible or convenient to have a conductor, and some scheme must be devised whereby the celebrant can himself do all that is required. One question, however, will almost certainly arise: "Ought such a training- or teaching-Eucharist to be an extra celebration, or can it be combined with that to which the majority of communicants come?" The answer must be determined by the circumstances of the parish. Temporarily to turn the 8 a.m. celebration or the 11 o'clock sung Eucharist into a teaching or training service might be difficult and undesirable, as many worshippers would probably feel such a scheme to be out of place. In

[1] See page 94.

The Structure of the Liturgy

Justin Martyr	The Prayer Book	
"And on the day called Sunday, all who live in cities or in the country gather together to one place, and the *memoirs of the apostles or the writings of the prophets are read*, as long as time permits; then, when the reader has ceased, the president *verbally instructs, and exhorts to the imitation of these good things.*	Lord's Prayer Collect for Purity " The Law " Kyries Collect ⎫ Epistle ⎬ Special for each Sunday and Holy-day. Gospel ⎭ Creed Sermon	PREPARATION
Then *we all rise together* and *pray*, and . . . when our prayer is ended, *bread and wine and water are brought,*	*Offering of :—* BREAD and WINE Alms Prayer for the Churchs Confession Absolution Comfortable Words	OFFERTORY
and *the president in like manner offers prayers and thanksgivings* according to his ability, *and the people assent* *saying Amen;*	"Lift up your hearts" (Prefaces for the Feasts) Sanctus Prayer of Humble Access CONSECRATION	CONSECRATION
and *there is a distribution made to each, and a participation.*"	THE COMMUNION	COMMUNION
	Lord's Prayer Thanksgiving Gloria Blessing	THANKSGIVING

This analysis is of the 1662 Rite as it stands,[1] and can easily be adapted to any permissible deviations or additions that obtain in particular parishes.

---

[1] Except for the omission of the Collect for the King (as 1928).

such cases there would have to be a separate celebration for the purpose of training the catechumens. But where there is a 9 or 9.30 Parish Communion it can easily be made into a teaching Eucharist for a short period, say the six Sundays of Lent, without undue disturbance, and many worshippers of experience would value such a ' refresher course '.

The plan outlined below has been used with some success and can readily be adapted to varying circumstances. It consists simply in selecting one aspect of the Eucharist each Sunday and emphasising it by means of explanation, hymns, biddings and action. The only variation from the normal order is that on the first two Sundays the address is given before the service begins. On the remaining four the sermon occupies its proper place, after the Creed. Special prominence may be given to each of the three acts, Offertory, Consecration and Communion, by prefacing them with a very brief bidding and/or the singing of one or two verses of an appropriate hymn. Thus:

OFFERTORY. "As we present the bread and wine, together with our alms, upon the altar we will sing . . ."

CONSECRATION. "As we come to the most solemn act of Consecration let us sing, kneeling . . ."

COMMUNION. " Before we draw near to receive the holy sacrament of our Lord's Body and Blood, we will sing as an act of faith and love . . ."

The addresses are given in outline only. The hymns suggested are from the *English Hymnal* and from *Ancient and*

This collect is not without liturgical precedent, though it should properly be said *after* the Collect of the day. But as the King is (quite rightly) prayed for in the Prayer for the Church, a special collect at this point seems logically and devotionally out of place. It should be remembered, however, that the King is anointed and consecrated by the Church to be her protector and governor. For a full discussion of the subject, see the essay on " The Regalism of the Prayer-book " in *Some Principles and Services of the Prayer-book*, J. Wickham Legg (Rivingtons, 1899).

Modern. Where the same hymn occurs in both books, this is indicated by an = sign. Otherwise alternatives are given.

Note.—The hymn for the Consecration is in each case intended to be sung immediately after the Comfortable Words.

First Sunday. Address before the Service begins

OUR LORD'S OWN SERVICE

For the next six Sundays we are going to try to increase our understanding of and devotion to this great central act of Christian worship, the Holy Communion or Eucharist. Each Sunday we shall concentrate on one aspect of this holy mystery, so that by entering more deeply into the meaning of each part we may come to grasp more fully the meaning and wonder of the whole.

We must begin by remembering that this great Sacrament that we are about to celebrate is not the invention or discovery of men, however good. It has come to us by our Lord's own gift and command. Let us think about this.

(*Reading.*) St. Luke xxii. 1–2, 7–13. Why all this mystery? Our Lord was now virtually a hunted man, safe in the protection afforded by the crowd during the day, but in danger from his enemies when alone and at night. It was the strength of his determination to secure undisturbed this last meal with his disciples that made him chose this means of keeping their meeting-place a secret. " With desire I have desired (*i.e.*, I have earnestly desired) to eat this Passover with you before I suffer." Here was something of evident importance to our Lord, something he took great pains to ensure that his disciples should *do* after he had left them : " This do in remembrance of me ". What is this that we are to do ? To do as he did. He *took* bread and wine. He *blessed* them. He *gave* to the disciples. That is what we do. Throughout the centuries the Eucharistic rite has always centred upon these three acts. First, bread and wine are placed on the altar (the Offertory). Second, the priest, speaking and acting for the whole congregation, blesses them (the Consecration). Third, they are distributed to the faithful (the Communion). The part of the service which comes before the Eucharistic action is a preparation; that which follows it is a thanksgiving.

We shall mark each of these three acts by singing one or two verses of a hymn immediately before it, but we shall remember that these three acts are all part of *one action* which we are bidden to perform out of loyalty to our Lord and in remembrance of his Passion. "As often as ye eat this bread and drink this cup, ye do shew the Lord's death till he come."

Let us think, then, today of this great truth. This is the Lord's own service. Whatever may be our difficulties, failures or misunderstandings, we are invited by our Lord to break this bread and share this cup. The initiative lies not with us, but with him. We do not come *primarily* because we need his grace, but because he bids us come. Whoever stays away, he is here. This is his feast. We are the guests. He is Host. We come to meet him.

		E. H.	A. M.
HYMNS	Offertory	334, vv. 1, 2 =	321, vv. 1, 3.
	Consecration	300, vv. 1, 2 or 718	
	Communion	306, v. 4	or 323, vv. 1, 2.

Second Sunday. Address before the Service begins.

PREPARATION

Last Sunday we were thinking of the fact that the three-fold action of the Eucharist is carried out in obedience to our Lord's command. Naturally we shall want to obey not in the spirit of a slave who does only the minimum required, but with all the love and reverence we can bring. Just because it is our Lord who bids us come, we shall prepare and make ready our coming. In the Prayer-Book service there are two acts of preparation. We may think of the first as *universal* (because it has always been part of the Eucharistic rite), and of the second as *special* (because devotional impulse has added it to our Prayer-Book service).

The universal preparation or introduction is that part of the service which comes before the Offertory. In the early Church those who were being prepared for baptism were only allowed to stay for this preparatory part (the Missa Cate-chumenorum as distinct from the Missa Fidelium). It consists of :

The Lord's Prayer.	A relic of the Priest's Preparation.
The Collect for Purity.	"That we may worthily" worship.
The Reading of the Law.	By which Christians are to rule their lives.
The Kyries.	"Lord, have mercy" (and incline our hearts to keep this law).
The Collect.	The special prayer for the day.
The Epistle.	Usually part of a letter from one of the Apostles about the Christian life.
The Gospel.	The words and actions of our Lord himself. (That is why we stand.)
The Creed.	The profession of our faith. Cf. soldiers saluting the flag. (The sign of the Cross at the end is a way of saying 'Amen',

or endorsing our Creed "in token that hereafter we may not be ashamed to confess the faith of Christ crucified, but manfully to fight," etc.)

The Sermon.

The only place at which a sermon is appointed to be preached at one of the regular services. Hence it is assumed that all the faithful in the parish will be present. After to-day the sermon will be preached in its proper place. (The printing in full of the three exhortations provided as alternatives to the sermon somewhat confuses the clarity of the arrangement of the service.)

All this is an obvious and fitting introduction to the Eucharistic action which is to follow. It proclaims the standards of the Christian life and prays that we may more worthily offer our worship.

The second or special act of preparation, the one that is peculiar to our Prayer-Book, comes immediately and appropriately before the Consecration. It consists of:

"Ye that do truly. . . ."
The Confession and Absolution.
The Comfortable Words.

The Prayer of Humble Access, which is properly a part of this special and immediate preparation, is inserted between the Sanctus and the Consecration Prayer (an unusual arrangement). But the meaning and intention of it all are perfectly clear. Before we draw near to our Lord in his Sacramental

Presence we confess our sins, receive absolution and the assurance of the efficacy of his Sacrifice for the salvation of sinners. It is true that " we are not worthy so much as to gather up the crumbs " under our Lord's Table. But it is equally true that " Christ Jesus came into the world to save sinners ".

Last Sunday we thought of our Lord's command. Today we shall think especially of our response, and try to make it the best that we can. It is not a question of feelings. We are not asked to *feel* our Lord's Presence; to *feel* our unworthiness; to *feel* the sacredness of this Sacrament. We are asked to obey; to accept; to believe. But just because we come in faith, we must examine ourselves before we come, and prepare ourselves as fully as we can.

		E. H.	*A. M.*
	Offertory	309, vv. 1, 2, 4 =	663, vv. 1, 2, 3.
HYMNS	Consecration	318, vv. 1, 2	or 717.
	Communion	307, v. 1 =	313, vv. 1, 2.

Third Sunday.   Address after the Creed

THE OFFERTORY

The Sermon (when there is one) is the concluding part of the Introduction or Preparation. Immediately afterwards the Eucharistic drama proper begins. Bread and wine are placed on the altar. This represents the first of our Lord's three actions : he *took*, he *blessed*, he *gave*.

We were thinking last Sunday of the fact that before we draw near to our Lord in his Sacramental Presence we must prepare ourselves to meet him. This first part of the Eucharistic rite is a symbolic gathering up of all our preparation in an act which not only expresses our complete dependence upon God, but also signifies that we come to him without reservation, bringing the whole of our lives. This will be clear if we think of the significance of these two simple things—bread and wine.

What is bread ? It is ' the staff of life '; that by which we live and for which we earn our wages. Cf. ' earning our bread and cheese '. It is the symbol of the greater part of our human activity, since we spend so much of our energy and time in providing for the necessities of life. Think, as Studdert Kennedy used to say, of that little piece of bread or pure white wafer. What is it ?

Where has it come from ? Maybe from Canada or the Argentine, where the corn ripened and was gathered. It was brought across the seas in the giant ships which are the products of our vast industrial civilisation, and manned by a host of men, sailors, stokers and engineers. By the time the corn has become flour and the flour has been made into bread it has in it not only symbolically but actually a world of human labour and genius. The gloom and darkness of the mine, the throb of the engines, the flames of the furnace, the dust of the mill, the heat of the bakery—all are there. It is these, the whole of our common life and work, that are offered to God upon the altar under the symbol of bread.

The wine is the juice of the grape, the token of all God's gifts to us in nature; potatoes, pears and plums, the cabbage-patch, the allotment and the farm. All these are offered to God under the symbol of wine. Father's work in the factory, mother's care for the family at home, Joan's work at the hospital and John's new job in the office—all the daily toil and joys of men and women, their daily bread and the means whereby they earn it, all the gifts of God to men in creation, all that goes to make up our human life is represented by the bread and the wine, and offered upon the altar to God.

> All that we have we offer,
> For it is all thine own,
> All gifts, by thine appointment,
> In bread and cup are shown.

In earlier days, members of the congregation actually brought to church the bread and wine and other gifts which were presented at the altar with much ceremony. Traces of this custom still remain—*e.g.*, at Milan the bread and the wine-cruets are brought up by the old men and women who live in the almshouses attached to the Cathedral. Today we find it more convenient to bring money. But the real ' offertory ' is that which is symbolised by all three of these gifts—namely, our whole lives, " ourselves, our souls and bodies ", which, as we shall remember next Sunday, are soon to be offered to God in union with our Lord's perfect offering.

It is the whole body, the whole congregation (indeed, the whole Body of Christ), that offers. (Hence the server who is the representative of the lay-folk within the sanctuary.) We act together, offering ourselves, and our prayers for " the whole state of Christ's Church ", and we receive back from our Lord's hands the symbols of that offering filled with his Sacramental Presence and Life.

By this action, then, we acknowledge our dependence upon God, and his claim upon the whole of our lives. Our Lord gave and revealed himself to his disciples because when he called them they were prepared to follow him whole-heartedly, putting the whole of their lives (money, work, time) at his disposal. To remind ourselves that it is nothing less than this that we should desire to give him, and in order to emphasise that this is what the Offertory means, the bread and wine will be brought up with the alms from the back of the church. (We shall continue to do this for the next three Sundays.) Here, if anywhere, is the lie to the idea that there is any such thing as a religious ' department ' of life. Let us, then, present our offerings to the Lord, with reverence and godly fear.

		E. H.	*A. M.*
Hymns	Offertory	334, vv. 1, 2	or 712.
	Consecration	318, vv. 1, 2	or 717.
	Communion	320, vv. 1, 2	= 317, vv. 1, 2.

Note.—If the practice of bringing up the elements from the back of the church is to be continued during the course, it may help to emphasise its meaning if each communicant is given a wafer as he enters, which he himself puts into the ciborium, conveniently placed for the purpose.

Fourth Sunday.   *Address after the Creed*

THE CONSECRATION

Some of you may have wondered why during these last three Sundays we have sung the hymn used to mark the beginning of the Consecration before the " Lift up your hearts " (*Sursum Corda*), and not before the Consecration Prayer itself.   We have done this because the *Sursum Corda is* the beginning of the Consecration.   It is, in fact, one of the oldest known parts of the Eucharist rite (*c.* A.D. 220), and has always been used at the beginning of the Consecration to commemorate the fact that before our Lord " blessed and brake " he " gave thanks ".   It is only in our Prayer Book that the Prayer of Humble Access is put between this thanksgiving (*Sursum*, Preface and *Sanctus*) and the Prayer of Consecration.   Yet it is an arrangement that is devotionally suitable and satisfying.   The nearer we approach to our Lord the more acutely conscious we become of our unworthiness and sinfulness.   It is surely right that we should say :

" We do not presume to come to this thy Table, O merciful Lord, trusting in our own righteousness, but in thy manifold and great mercies. . . ."

H

This is the truth that we must think about today. We are not worthy. Last Sunday we were thinking of the fact that in the Offertory we offer to God the daily life and work, plans, interests and talents of every one of us. To offer is the essence of worship. Yet we cannot but be conscious that our lives are far from being a perfect offering. God alone knows just how imperfect they are. We want to offer him the best, yet our best is not nearly good enough. What is to be done ? Here we come to the heart of the Christian faith and of the Eucharistic mystery. There *is* one offering " full, perfect and sufficient "—and only one—the perfect life and complete obedience, even to death, of our Lord Jesus Christ. What we can do, therefore, is to put our sin-stained, unworthy and trivial little offering into the perfect offering (' sacrifice ' = offering) of our Lord, and pray :

> Look, Father, look on his anointed face,
>   And only look on us as found in him ;
> Look not on our misusings of thy grace,
>   Our prayer so languid, and our faith so dim :
> For lo ! between our sins and their reward
>   We set the Passion of thy Son our Lord.

The Eucharist is rooted in the Passion and sacrificial death of our Lord. "As often as ye eat this bread and drink this cup, ye do shew forth the Lord's death till he come." All that he came on earth to do is here portrayed, and by this divinely appointed means we receive " remission of our sins and all other benefits of his Passion ". (It is almost impossible to avoid using the actual words of the Communion Office, so exactly do they express the great truths of this holy mystery.)

Let us, then, think today of the life and death of our Lord, and of the salvation he has wrought for mankind. Let us offer to him our whole lives, and pray that they, together with these simple gifts of bread and wine, may be sanctified by his Grace, and filled with his Presence and Power.

$$E.\,H. \qquad\qquad A.\,M.$$

HYMNS $\begin{cases} \text{Offertory} & 335 & \text{or } 714. \\ \text{Consecration} & 302,\text{ vv. } 1,\,2 & = 322,\text{ vv. } 1,\,2. \\ \text{Communion} & 302,\text{ v. } 4 & = 322,\text{ v. } 4. \end{cases}$

Fifth Sunday.   *Address after the Creed*

THE COMMUNION

The act of Communion is the climax of the three-fold Eucharistic drama: he took, he blessed, he *gave*. The bread and wine which we have offered on the altar are given back to us having been blessed or consecrated by the words and action of our Lord himself. The lives and work that we have brought are sanctified and redeemed by his sacrificial life and death.

All down the ages Christians have known that in this holy Sacrament they have come into the Presence of Christ himself and have shared his life in a manner that is possible by no other means. Exactly *how* our Lord fulfils his own words " This is my body ", " This is my blood ", we cannot know. We only know that under this outward sign, as the Catechism says, the Body and Blood of Christ " are verily and indeed taken and received by the faithful ".

" Yes," some people may say, " but the bread is still mere bread, and the wine is still ordinary wine." Is it? Is a wedding ring *merely* a piece of gold? If so, why should a woman be so distressed when she loses her wedding ring? She can easily obtain another.

" But," you say, " it would not be the same. It would not be her *wedding* ring; it would not be the ring her husband placed on her finger when they were married." Exactly. The wedding ring certainly remains what it has always been—a piece of gold. But it is now something more than mere gold. It has acquired a new significance. How much 'more' than mere bread and wine, then, is that heavenly food which our Lord places in our hands. No one imagines that the bread and wine have become our Lord's *physical* flesh and blood. But they have become his Body and Blood *spiritually*; *significantly*; *sacramentally*. That is what the Prayer-Book teaches and what the Church has always believed.

What, after all, is a 'body'? Your body is the means by which you communicate yourself to other people, by which you express yourself to them and come into contact with them. So our Lord's Sacramental Body is that by which, in this holy rite, he meets with us and communicates himself to us.

Holy Scripture nowhere encourages us to think of God's presence and activity in a vague, nebulous manner. He reveals himself to men and acts towards them at definite times and in definite places; supremely in his Incarnation in the reign of Caesar Augustus in the land we call Palestine. So our Lord is not vaguely and nebulously present to his disciples. When two or three are gathered together in his Name, he is in the midst of them. In the blessed bread and wine he is personally and really present, and in this sacramental mode he gives himself and his life to his faithful disciples.

		E. H.		*A. M.*
	Offertory	320, vv. 1, 2	=	317, vv. 1, 2.
HYMNS	Consecration	307, v. 1	=	313, vv. 1, 2 or 715, vv. 1, 2.
	Communion	304	=	318.

Sixth Sunday. Address after the Creed

THE THANKSGIVING

We have thought together of the three-fold cycle of the Eucharistic action. First, the Offertory, in which we offer to God our lives and work under the symbols of bread and wine. Second, the Consecration, by which our unworthy offering is *put into* the perfect Sacrifice of our Lord, and the simple elements are made by him into the vehicles by which he gives himself to us. Third, the Communion or sharing together in the sacramental Life and Grace which Christ bestows upon us by this his own appointed means. Our daily lives have been brought, transformed and given back to us. It is a perfect cycle or rhythm embracing the three great acts of God for man—Creation, Incarnation and Redemption.

Yet if the Eucharistic Office ended with the Communion (as it does in the Roman Church), we should feel that something was missing. We should want to say " Thank you ". Thanksgiving is a very important element in the Sacrament of Holy Communion. Hence the old name ' Eucharist ', which is the Greek word for thanksgiving. (Cf. " when he had *given thanks*, he brake it, and gave it to his disciples "). We may well be grateful that our Prayer-Book makes such full provision for thanksgiving, more than do most of the great Liturgies.

The first thing, therefore, that we do after making our Communion is to say together the great prayer of all Christians, " Our Father ". Then follows a thanksgiving prayer, the *Gloria* and the Blessing. The celebration is over. We have shared in the most holy and sacred mystery known to man. We have partaken of the sacramental Body and Blood of Christ. We go our several ways to " shew forth his praise not only with our lips but with our lives ". We go back to our homes and offices and workshops and markets, there to bear our witness to the Christ whom we have received. (No man can receive Christ without gaining also a deepened desire to bring other men to him. For that is Christ's desire, and where he is that longing must also be present.)

Yet there is an important sense in which our Eucharist is not finished, and never will be in this life. For just as in each Eucharist our sin-stained lives are offered, sanctified and received back, so the same three-fold cycle is worked out from one Eucharist to the next. We receive Christ; we go forth strengthened by his Presence; we return bringing our sins and failures and receiving fresh Grace and Life.

> Jesus said, "I am the living bread which came down from heaven: if any man eat of this bread, he shall live for ever; yea, and the bread which I will give is my flesh, for the life of the world."

		E. H.	A. M.
HYMNS	Offertory	309, vv. 1, 2, 4 =	663, vv. 1, 2, 3.
	Consecration	335	or 720, vv. 1, 2.
	Communion	307	= 313, vv. 1, 2.
	Thanksgiving	424 or 329	665 or 316.

There are doubtless many ways in which such a scheme may be improved and amended. It is not suggested that the addresses outlined above represent a complete summary of Eucharistic teaching, or that they will appear satisfactory to every reader.[1] They are only intended to illustrate a *modus*

---

[1] *E.g.*, some may feel that since in the Liturgy of 1662 the Prayer of Oblation *follows* the Communion, we should teach that it is only after receiving our Lord's Life that we are worthy to " offer ourselves our souls and bodies ". It may also be argued that the phrase " alms and oblations " was not intended by the revisers of 1662 to refer to anything other than the money offerings. (Bishop John Dowden in *Further Studies in the Prayer Book*; Methuen,

operandi of helping those who (though they have already had some sacramental teaching) are on the threshold of their sacramental life to understand something of the meaning and the movement of the Liturgy. Quite apart from the training of the Catechumens, such an occasional Teaching Eucharist might be a welcome and useful addition to the religious education of a parish.

The practical difficulty presented by the printing of the three Exhortations after the Prayer for the Church in the standard editions of the Prayer-Book can easily be overcome by purchasing copies of the Communion Service in which this somewhat confusing arrangement is rectified.[1] The *Church-people's Prayer Book*, published for the Church in Wales,[2] is an excellent example of sensible and clear laying out of the subject-matter with the minimum of deviations from the standard edition.

The importance of stressing the three-fold action of the Eucharist is that it gives the rightful prominence to the Offertory. There has been great loss in the almost exclusive emphasis frequently laid on ' receiving Communion '. That Communion is the centre and climax of the Sacrament is not questioned. But the presentation of the Eucharist solely in terms of ' food for our souls ' is not only to neglect the important truth of oblation, but also to leave unanswered the question, " How is it that so many people seem to be

---

1908, adduces strong historical evidence in support of this thesis.) Though such an argument still leaves unexplained why, if the revisers had no intention of following ancient liturgical precedent, they directed that the elements should be placed on the altar *at this point*, and not before the service begins.

In any case, the difference is more apparent than real. Though the treatment outlined above follows traditional Eucharistic teaching and practice, either interpretation safeguards the truth that our imperfect offering is made in union with our Lord's perfect sacrifice, and in the power of the redemption he has wrought for us.

[1] An excellent edition is published by S.P.C.K. at 2*d.* each.
[2] By Messrs. Snowden & Co., Monmouth.

able to do without Communion ? ". The answer to many
of the criticisms made by people today about the gulf
between religion and everyday life is to recover for the
Offertory its rightful place in our Eucharistic teaching and
worship.

CHAPTER V

MORNING AND EVENING PRAYER

WHEN we come to the subject of Morning and Evening Prayer we are faced with an initial difficulty in that not only has Sunday Mattins come to be elevated to a position of importance never envisaged by the compilers of the Prayer-Book, but both Sunday Mattins and Evensong have come to serve a purpose quite different from that for which they were designed. According to the purpose of the compilers of the Prayer-Book, the chief Sunday morning service was the Holy Communion, to which Mattins was quite rightly regarded as preparatory. It proved impossible, however, to carry out their ideal. Though the Eucharist was still celebrated after Morning Prayer, the celebrations became infrequent, and Mattins was removed to a later hour of the morning. Religion became less concerned with the redemption of the world by our Lord Jesus Christ than with respectability, good form and the Establishment. Communion came to be the prerogative of the gentry. The nineteenth-century attempt to restore the habit of more frequent communion by the introduction of the early celebration did not, however, succeed in disturbing the central place that Mattins had come to occupy on Sunday morning. Morning Prayer and Holy Communion became divorced at the expense and to the detriment of the Eucharist as the chief act of Sunday morning worship. But the addition of hymns, a sermon, and, later, the blessing, gradually upset the balance and changed the emphasis both of Morning and of Evening Prayer. The extent of this transformation may be seen to-day in the fact that for a very large proportion of Church worshippers the 'high lights' of the service are the

hymns and the sermon. To these popular additions the
office as a whole has become subordinate. If hymns and
sermon are unattractive or inappropriate, the service as a
whole is regarded as having missed the mark. When there
is any question of shortening or modifying the service, it is
the Psalms and Lessons which are selected for reduction or
omission, never the hymns or the sermon.

It would be pedantic in the extreme to suggest that these
popular additions to Sunday Morning and Evening Prayer
were misguided, or to deny that they have been of devotional
value to thousands of people. So long as the majority of
people in the parish had sufficient grasp of the elements of
the Christian religion to enable them to find in Mattins and
Evensong adequate vehicles of popular devotion, the addition
of sermon and hymns to assist this devotion was justified.
But now that the vast mass of people have become so
religiously ignorant that they want to forsake the ancient
liturgical building and live in the modern annexe, it is clearly
time to consult the architect's plans and to ask whether the
parent structure is capable of any further additions without
complete annihilation, or whether a separate building should
not be erected temporarily to shelter the homeless. Experience should also warn us that shortage of suitable accommoda-
tion offers dangerous scope to the slum landlord and the
jerry-builder.

We have to choose between three courses of action :

1. So to modify and modernise Mattins and Evensong
that they are unrecognisable as such.

2. To regard them as out-moded, and to offer instead
a popular substitute ' revelant ' to modern conditions.

3. To regard them as providing a norm and standard
of Anglican worship, which (with certain minor modifications) are as effective an expression of worship for
this age as for any other, and to face the need for

training the un-instructed to appreciate and use them properly.

It is to be hoped that even the most sceptical reader (if he has persevered thus far) will be persuaded that there is at least a strong case to be made for the third of these choices.

We have already considered a method by which the non-churchgoer who has become a ' hearer ' or catechumen may be initiated into the use of some of the acts or parts, the raw material, as it were, of Morning and Evening Prayer. The next step (and it is not a difficult one) will be to enable the ' hearer ' to see these parts in relation to the whole. But the question at once arises, " To what whole ? " The whole exactly as defined in 1662, or 1928, or the whole as it has come in general usage to be ? Further, if ' general usage ' be allowed, what is to prevent the growth of a usage which will gradually transform Morning and Evening Prayer into something that bears no relation whatever to the Prayer-Book services ? What modifications may be regarded as loyal and legitimate, and which should be condemned as being neither ?

Let us examine the common criticisms of Mattins and Evensong made by many clergy and lay-folk. It is said that :

1. The Psalms and Lessons are usually too long. The Old Testament Lessons are often obscure, and those from the New Testament frequently contain too much subject-matter for rapid digestion.

2. The ' Church and State ' prayers are not a very edifying example of Christian intercession, and are far too restricted in their scope.

3. The sermon, which does at least provide the preacher with an opportunity of directing the minds of his congregation towards God, comes too late in the service for such directed thinking to be expressed in prayer and worship within the framework of the service.

4. Invariably to begin the service with the General Confession seems unreal to many, because they do not feel ' miserable ' and are not quite convinced that they are ' sinners '. (" They haven't done anyone any harm " !)

In actual practice, however, the first three of these difficulties are frequently overcome because :

1. Many clergy choose their own Sunday Lessons. (There is no authority for this practice, which often degenerates into a constant repetition of certain well-known passages. The same is true of the Psalms.)

2. Most Bishops allow their clergy considerable latitude in their choice of intercessions, etc., after the Third Collect, and in point of fact prayers are in common use drawn from a wide variety of sources.

3. It is becoming increasingly customary to preach the sermon after the Third Collect, and to follow it with such special prayers as are thought appropriate.

The Sunday Lessons present many problems. Though the habit of mind which tends to discard the Lectionary in favour of a few favourite chapters constantly repeated is to be deplored, there are many conscientious parish priests who in the best interests of their people frequently feel driven to reject the set lessons as unsuitable. It is a pity that such men should be placed in the position of having to choose between duty to their people and loyalty to authority. The Lectionary of 1922 as revised in 1928 is certainly a vast improvement on its predecessor. The recognition that the Sunday lesson-scheme must be arranged independently of the daily lessons was an obvious necessity. But the compilers still appear to have laboured under the delusion that the bulk of church people attend Mattins *and* Evensong *every* Sunday. This is true of a very small minority only. A large proportion of those who attend Sunday Evensong do not go to Mattins at all, and many of those who attend Mattins never go to church in the evening. There is great need for a lectionary which recognises this fact, and arranges the morning and evening Lessons independently. At the same time the Lessons could be shortened with considerable advantage.

Yet the principle of a system which provides worshippers with at least a conspectus of Holy Scripture during the course of any one year is that which guided the compilers of our Prayer-Book,[1] and it is one to which the preferences of the individual priest should never be allowed to become subordinate. The tremendous difficulty of compiling a lectionary which can achieve this purpose in fifty-two reasonably short lessons drawn from each Testament, while a strong argument in favour of a three-year scheme such as is in use in the Episcopal Church in Scotland, should dispose clergy to be a little less impatient with the Lectionary than they are sometimes wont to be. On the whole it would seem that the wisest and most loyal policy is to adhere to the Revised Lectionary, unless there are extremely cogent reasons for occasional departure from it.[2]

The same is true of the Psalter. The use of the Psalms for the day of the month on Sundays is very appropriate for the clergy and such few of the faithful laity who go through the Psalter each month. But for the majority, who only come to Evensong on Sundays, this practice entirely defeats its purpose. The provision of a table of Psalms for Sundays and Holy Days in the 1928 Prayer-Book has filled a long-felt want, and where its use is sanctioned by the Diocesan there is now no excuse for not following it faithfully.

Quite apart, however, from Psalms, Lessons, hymns and sermon, there are few churches where the strict letter of the 1662 offices is followed exactly. For example, it is now the

[1] Vide *Concerning the Service of the Church.*
[2] A Committee of Convocation is at work on the Sunday Lessons and will probably report soon.

exception rather than the rule to hear the opening exhortation
read in full.   The same is true of the five prayers which
follow the Third Collect.   Over a period of years changes
are gradually introduced which become accepted as the
norm.   That such gradual and generally accepted change is
not in itself inconsistent with loyal Anglicanism is made
clear in the Preface to the Book of Common Prayer :

> " It hath been the wisdom of the Church of England,
> ever since the first compiling of her publick Liturgy, to
> keep the mean between the two extremes, of too much
> stiffness in refusing, and of too much easiness in
> admitting any variation from it."

At the same time it is necessary to ensure that changes,
however gradually introduced, do not become inconsistent
with that sound and balanced Catholic theology which,
through many vicissitudes, it has been the genius of the
Prayer Book to preserve.   To shorten the exhortation and to
add some further intercessions involve no such fundamental
change in the purpose or theology of Mattins and Evensong
as would be the case if the Confession or Old Testament
Lesson were omitted and the Psalms were to be chosen
haphazard by the minister.   The Confession safeguards
the truth that we come before God as sinners who need
redemption, and not as equal co-promoters with God of
human blessedness.   The regular and ordered reading of
the Psalms and Old Testament scriptures preserves the
perspective which enables us to see ourselves as part of that
redemptive purpose of God, wrought out in human history
through the Israel of old to the new man in Christ.

The attempt so to modify Morning and Evening Prayer
as to make them into ' popular ' services, tempered to the
erroneous presuppositions of this generation, can only end
in theological and liturgical disaster.   Their structure does
not lend itself to such treatment.   Let them remain what

they are, worship for the instructed Christian, and let us face the need for training our people to use them properly. How many of the clergy who take it upon themselves to ' brighten up ' Mattins or Evensong have ever tried to train their people in the right use and understanding of these offices ? It may well be that in due course alternative services will be drawn up by competent liturgical scholars, and issued under authority. Until that time comes there is no need for any priest to regard the Prayer Book services as a restrictive handicap to evangelistic endeavour. If some such method of initiation into the various parts of these services (General Confession, Versicles and Responses, the phraseology of the Psalms, Creed, and Canticles, etc.) described in the foregoing chapters has been adopted, it will not be a far cry to the use of the services in full. There only remains the task of helping people to understand their liturgical movement and structure.

One further problem, however, arises with regard to Mattins. The number of clergy who desire to see Mattins retained as the main service of Sunday morning diminishes every year. What, then, is to become of Mattins ?

Those who come only to the Sung Eucharist run the risk of devotional impoverishment in not hearing the Psalms and scriptures read ' in course ', though there is every reason for encouraging such people to read the Bible devotionally at home. The suggestion has sometimes been made that the Prayer Book order of Mattins followed by Holy Communion might still be maintained. If the sermon does not exceed fifteen minutes, the music is simple, and full advantage is taken of the omissions allowed in the 1928 Book, the whole can be completed in one hour and ten minutes without unseemly haste.[1] Those who are not willing or able to attend for the whole time can come in quietly during the *Benedictus*, or leave during the offertory hymn. Some such

[1] Vide an article " The Problem of the Sunday Services " by Dr. Lowther Clarke in *Theology*, July 1929.

plan may be the answer to the problem. Certainly it would be wrong for a newly inducted vicar to deprive of Mattins those who have grown up to regard it as their proper vehicle of worship. However right may be his desire to make the Eucharist the chief service, his method of approach to this end in a parish of Mattins tradition must be by addition, and not by subtraction. Whether Mattins should in such a case be before, or, as it often is, after the Sung Eucharist or Parish Communion can only be decided, in this transition stage, by the circumstances of the particular parish. To generalise about the question of times of Sunday morning services would be foolish. But it is likely that 11 a.m. will become less and less popular or convenient in the future.

At least this much may be said about Sunday Mattins. Whether we are considering the faithful who have been brought up in the Mattins tradition and are now too old and too set in their ways to change, or the faithful Eucharistic worshippers, to whose offering the addition of Mattins as a preparation might be devotionally valuable—the need is for training in its proper use. In the case of the former there is everything to be gained by helping them to make a more worshipful use of the office (even to trying to show them that it is *not* the Church's chief act of worship on Sunday morning !), and everything to be lost by bowdlerising it into a popular sing-song coupled with a dose of uplift.

There are, however, two changes which in the interests of intelligibility and teaching value might well be made in the present lay-out of Mattins. Whereas Evensong has a logical and chronological movement, in that the Old and New Testament Lessons are linked together by the *Magnificat* (see " Evensong-Training Experiment " below), and followed by the *Nunc Dimittis*, Mattins upsets this reproduction of the Bible story by inserting the *Te Deum*, a Christian hymn, before the New Testament Lesson. The *Benedictus*, which is a historical link between the Old Testament and the

Incarnation, is sung after the second lesson. Clearly this order should be reversed. Why should not permission be sought to sing the *Benedictus* between the two Lessons, and the *Te Deum* after the second Lesson ? If to this interchange were added permission to omit the eight versicles and responses which formed no part of the original hymn, so that the *Te Deum* ended, as properly it does, at " Make them to be numbered with Thy saints in glory everlasting", the logic of Mattins would be as perfect as that of Evensong. It follows, of course, that the custom of substituting the *Benedicite* for the *Te Deum* during Lent would have to cease. This alternative was ordered in the first Prayer Book of Edward VI, but in subsequent editions has been left optional. There is nothing to be said for making use of the option, except by making Lent unnecessarily penitential at the expense of significance. Its length and monotonous form make it unsuitable for modern use. Neither is there any- thing to be said for making use of any of the alternative canticles. The *Benedictus* and *Te Deum*, the *Magnificat* and *Nunc Dimittis* should be regarded as fixed parts of Mattins and Evensong. Their content, and in the case of the three New Testament songs their origin, makes them uniquely suitable for their normal function in the Daily Offices, and they should on no account be varied.

The problems that surround the place and purpose of Sunday Mattins do not, fortunately, arise in the case of Evensong. Evensong is enshrined in affectionate regard in the hearts of the majority of church-people, and though the 1928 Prayer Book's revival of Compline is greatly to be welcomed, it is unlikely that it will ever become a rival to Evensong. Partly because it is the service of Sunday evening (and it is a fact that evening religion has more emotional associations than has the morning), and partly because of its close association with the story of our Lord's birth, Evensong is popular with many who find Mattins cold and uninspiring.

I

The following account of a course designed to train a congregation in the art of Evensong worship may, perhaps, illustrate both the principle described in Chapter III, and also the method of linking up the 'raw material' of the office to its movement and structure. It is based on the fact that Evensong tells the story of the Incarnation, and makes use of the sermon to introduce the particular part or stage of Evensong which is to be studied. The sermon therefore occurs at a different point in the service each Sunday, and the stage which it introduces follows immediately as the 'expression work'. The congregation is thus make to think about each of the various steps in the service *before* taking part in it. The style and method of presenting the subject-matter of the addresses must of course be determined by the conductor and by the needs of his congregation. A brief précis is given only of those sections of the addresses which it would be cumbersome to describe in indirect speech.

EVENSONG TRAINING COURSE

1st *Sunday*.

Omitting the General Confession and beginning with the Our Father, Evensong, is sung as usual up to the Third Collect, after which the Address is given (with or without an intervening hymn).

> " For the next four Sundays we are going to try to make our worship on Sunday evenings more real and more intelligent by studying, more carefully than perhaps we have studied before, the service in which we have just taken part. Evening Prayer or Evensong is not just a random collection of prayers and psalms and lessons flung together like potatoes in a sack. It

is a perfect act of (non-sacramental) worship, and each of its parts is arranged to carry the worshipper steadily forward from the beginning to the climax. You see, Evensong tells a story—the story of the Incarnation—and each stage in the service is a fresh chapter in the story, carrying it forward step by step until it reaches its grand climax in the Creed.

"The first thing we do at Evensong is to say the General Confession. This is the Prologue to the story. It describes the situation in which we find ourselves when the story opens."

The address continues, explaining the nature of sin as man's age-long desire to be independent of God, to run his own life, and to be his own master. At the conclusion of the address the congregation is asked to kneel, and there follows a period of guided silence in which they are directed to consider and acknowledge the fact of sin, personal, social and national. The biddings need to be rather carefully worked out, making use here and there of phrases from the General Confession, which is finally said by the whole congregation as the summing up of the time of silence. After the Collect for Pardon, a hymn is sung, and the service ends with the usual prayers and the Blessing.

2nd Sunday.

On the second Sunday the preacher enters the pulpit at the beginning of the service and reminds the congregation of what they are going to do, and of what they have thought about the previous week—viz., that they are going to study Evensong; that Evensong tells a story—the story of the Incarnation—and that the General Confession is the Prologue to the story. The Confession is then said by the congregation, prefaced by the same biddings as on the previous Sunday. After the Absolution and Our Father the address is given:

" This being the human situation, man having sinned, having declared his independence of God, what is God to do about it ?   Is he to play the heavy father and force us to obey him ?   Or, on the other hand, will he leave us in ignorance of himself and his purpose ?   He did neither of these things.   God's method was quite amazing.   It was to become Incarnate ; to come to earth as man.   But this stupendous act of God involved considerable preparation—e.g., in the era immediately preceding the Incarnation the Romans and Greeks both combined unconsciously to prepare the world for the coming Gospel, the former by uniting the Mediterranean world under one rule, the latter by providing a common language.   But more important than this was the preparation of men's minds.   It would have been, humanly speaking, useless for God to have become Incarnate among people who believed that God was the ' man in the moon '.   Just therefore as God had endowed the Romans and Greeks each with a particular genius that was needed in the fulfilment of his age-long purpose, so he chose another race of men and endowed them with a unique religious genius, which enabled them to be peculiarly responsive to himself and his truth.   This ' peculiar people ' was the nation now known as the Jews."

(Here follows a brief summary of the part played by the Hebrew prophets and people) :

" How very right and natural, therefore, that the ' first chapter ' of Evensong should be the singing of some of the songs of ancient Israel, and the reading of some of their sacred writings."

The address concludes with a few sentences about the beauty of the Psalms, and their matchless expression of human aspiration after God, with particular reference to the two Psalms about to be sung.

The Old Testament Lesson is also prefaced with a short introduction, after which Evensong continues as usual, a hymn being sung in the place where the sermon normally occurs.

3rd Sunday.

On the third Sunday the same procedure is followed, and the story is carried one stage farther. The preacher enters the pulpit at the beginning of the service and reminds the congregation of what they have studied up to date, and prefaces the Confession ('The Prologue'), the Psalms and First Lesson (Chapter One) with brief introductions. The address is given after the Old Testament Lesson.

> "For generations, then, God had been preparing the world for his own coming, by choosing special nations and people each to play a particular part in making the world ready. Now, when the fulness of time was come, God chose an individual, Mary, daughter of Anna, to be the human vehicle by which his Incarnation should be wrought."

After a brief explanation of the place of the Blessed Virgin Mary in the Christian 'scheme' (commemorated by the Church every time we say the Nicene and Apostles' Creeds, or sing Evensong), the main part of the address is concerned with the meaning and implications of the Incarnation, linking together the *Magnificat*, the New Testament Lesson and the *Nunc Dimittis* as 'Chapter Two'. Each of these are then enacted with short introductions, and Evensong continues as usual.

4th Sunday.

On the fourth and last Sunday, before the service begins the preacher explains that whereas it has been necessary on

the previous Sundays to interrupt the continuity of the
service with explanations and biddings, today they are to
proceed right up to the end of the Second Lesson without
any further interruption. He reminds them of the logical
development of the story, Prologue, Chapters One and Two.
Evensong then begins. The address, which is given after
the New Testament Lesson, is on the subject of worship, and
it is explained that all prayer and all worship, being a response
to God, *must* begin with the recollection of God.

> " Its purpose is not to make ourselves more real to
> God, but to make God more real to us. Our primary
> concern is God, his will, and his purpose.
> " Just as in the pattern prayer of our Lord we think
> first of God—*thy* Name, *thy* kingdom, *thy* will—and
> afterwards of *our* daily bread, *our* sins, etc., so the whole
> of the first part of Evensong is taken up with God, and
> what God has done for us men and for our salvation.
> Each act of worship or scripture-reading carries forward
> the stupendous story of the Incarnation until it reaches
> its grand climax—its summary in the Creed. The
> Creed is the climax of the office, Chapter Three in our
> sequence. Then, and not till then, do we begin to
> think about our needs, asking God to bless our king,
> our people and to bring us through our wars.
> " Evensong is therefore a perfect act of Christian
> worship, which, so far from becoming dull by constant
> repetition, becomes ever more and more meaningful
> and expressive—so long, that is, as we remember what
> it is all about, and bring our own minds and wills into
> line with its spirit and movement."

The Creed is then said as a summary of the whole course,
and the usual intercessions follow.

It will, of course, be realised that such a treatment as that
described above is purely arbitrary, and made only in the

interests of teaching. It is unlikely that those who were responsible for the present form of Evensong consciously intended that it should tell the story of the Incarnation. But since, by happy chance or divine guidance, it does, it seems a pity not to utilise the fact, and even to make Mattins, by slight rearrangement, follow the same order.

This scheme was originally devised for the four Sundays of Advent. It could be made longer, and thus avoid the necessity of telescoping the *Magnificat*, Second Lesson and *Nunc Dimittis* together as ' Chapter Two '. Each might well have received separate treatment. On the other hand, such a course must not be spread out over so long a period that the sense of perspective is lost. Where the circumstances of the parish allow, it would be of great value if the last Sunday in the course could be given over to a ' Pageant of Evensong ', in which the various parts are presented dramatically—*e.g.*, some people, dressed to represent the pilgrims on their way to the Temple at Jerusalem, proceeding up the aisle during the singing of the (appropriate) psalms ; tableaux of Mary's visit to Elisabeth, of the manger scene, and of the Presentation of Christ in the Temple during the *Magnificat*, the Second Lesson, the *Nunc Dimittis* respectively.[1]

Matins would lend itself to similar treatment only if the *Te Deum* and *Benedictus* were interchanged, as suggested above.

In a village church a similar course was worked out for the six Tuesday evenings of Lent. But in this case Evensong was not sung in full till the last evening. On each of the other evenings the ' act ' studied was made the climax of the ' service '. The order was simple—hymn, talk followed by guided-silence, and finally summed up in the ' act ' or part considered. The parts thus treated were : 1. Confession.

[1] For a full description of the ' Pageant of Evensong ', see *The Child's Initiation*, by Phyllis Dent.

2. God and the people of Israel (Psalms and Old Testament Lesson). 3. The Incarnation (*Magnificat*). 4. The writing of the Epistles and Gospels (Second Lesson and *Nunc Dimittis*). 5. God's plan for Redemption of the world (The Creed). On the last evening the parts were put together and Evensong sung after the talk.

The Vicar of a parish in a northern industrial town writes :

> " In winter (for reasons of black-out, but we shall always continue the practice) we have the whole service of Evensong on lantern-slides. Pictures on the screen as people enter and depart give sufficient light by which to move about ; appropriate pictures—*e.g.*, of the crucifix, Madonna, etc.—are also shown during the Lessons and sermon. All kinds of slogans, notices, etc., are possible in frosted glass slides with ink writing. Sermons can be varied with lantern talks copiously illustrated."

The principle of *thinking* about a thing first (viz., during the address or sermon) and then *doing* it afterwards could be applied at Sunday Evensong in a manner which is in strict accordance with rubrical direction. The custom of preaching the sermon after the Third Collect, and the following it immediately (*i.e.*, without an intervening hymn) with biddings and silence leading into the general prayers and intercessions is wise, and though sometimes disliked by a few extremely conservative members of the congregation, is greatly appreciated by the majority. But since the logical ' act ' after some sermons is that of faith or worship, there would appear a strong argument for occasionally having the sermon earlier. The Prayer Book directs that the curate shall catechise the children after the Second Lesson at Evening Prayer. Why not put the sermon here sometimes ? There are many sermons (or ought to be) to which the *Nunc*

Dimittis, sung as an act of praise and thanksgiving, would be the most fitting ' expression work '.

Sometimes the sermon would come best between the *Nunc Dimittis* and the Creed.   The latter, prefaced by biddings and silences, would then be said with more significance and thoughtfulness than one suspects is frequently the case.

In one country church the vicar was faced with the difficulty that owing to the black-out he would have to hold Sunday evensong in the afternoon at the same hour as that at which his children's catechism class normally functioned. He decided to combine the two.   The children accordingly came to Evensong, and after the Third Collect were ' catechised '.   The grown-ups and parents did not put up their hands and volunteer any answers, but the fact that many of them said they found the ' catechism ' more instructive than the usual sermon, suggests that they made mental answers to the priest's questions, which they were able to compare (without revealing ignorance) with the answers worked out with the children.   The people now look forward to the autumn, when Evensong is put forward to the afternoon.

A further adaptation of this plan suggests itself.   Why, especially in the country, should we not follow the rubrical direction, and catechise the children after the Second Lesson at Evensong ?   The questions could be related to the subject-matter of the sermon, which would afterwards be given in its usual place.   Such a catechising could be used to most valuable purpose, if it stimulated questions in the minds of the adult members of the congregation by way of mental preparation for the sermon.

Some further practical suggestions for making Morning and Evening Prayer more intelligent and significant as acts of worship will be found in the Appendix.

CHAPTER VI

WORSHIP AND DRAMA

THIS chapter does not set out to be either a treatise on the dramatic element in religion or a study of the psychology of symbolism. Our sole concern is with the use of drama in evangelism and worship-training. We shall therefore begin by considering some of those modern mental attitudes and conditions which constitute something of a resistance to the acceptance of Christian truth, and then suggest ways and means by which drama and symbolism may be enlisted in the service of Christian teaching and training.

The first difficulty that faces the Christian preacher and teacher is the fact that no one can be argued into religion. Anyone who has had experience of evangelistic work knows that the method of reasoned argument, though it can be an effective weapon in breaking down the outer defences of ignorance and misunderstanding, has little or no converting power. One frequently meets people who have been intellectually convinced that on all reasonable and rational grounds the Christian Faith is true. But they hold back from personal committal to Christ. Their wills remain unmoved. Psychology has shown that we are much less creatures of reason than we like to think we are. Affection and imagination play a greater part in determining action than does reason, and often what seems to be 'pure reason' is conditioned by influences that are instinctive, emotional and irrational. Many a man has apparently sincere intellectual doubts about the truth of the Christian Faith. But behind those doubts, and largely responsible for them, there is an unwillingness to accept the Christian moral standard. It is at this point that evangelism must carry on where teaching and instruction leave off. The purpose of the latter is to inform the mind. Evangelism must be concerned to stimulate the will, and here the appeal to reason by itself is insufficient. The imagination and affections must be fired and the will moved.

A further problem is presented to the modern evangelist by the pseudo-scientific materialism of this present age. Contemporary education, with its lop-sided emphasis on the scientific approach, has tended to suggest that the only canons of truth are those of laboratory analysis or of statistics. That there should exist truth which is not discoverable by man, but can only be made known by the revelation of God, is a proposition which modern men and women find extraordinarily difficult to accept.

The following statement, made by a supposedly educated woman in the course of a discussion-group, though not distinguished for the intelligence it displays, is nevertheless typical of an attitude of mind that one is constantly meeting:

"How do you expect people to believe in Christianity today? Christianity depends on faith. But this is a scientific age, and we have learned to appreciate the importance of facts. What people need today is not faith, but fact."

It would, of course, be easy to reply that on its subjective or human side religious truth has been achieved by the same processes as scientific truth. The scientist begins with observed facts. These facts are then classified and a theory is evolved to account for them. This theory is then tested by experiment. If these experiments confirm the theory, and so long as subsequently discovered facts do not conflict with it, the theory is held to be 'true'. Religion likewise, on its subjective side, begins with and derives from facts of human experience. Christ was a fact in the experience of his followers, a fact to be accounted for. In one sense it can be said that the dogma of the Incarnation is a theory produced to account for the fact, and has been tested in the experience of thousands of Christians. But here the analogy breaks down. For the basic ' facts ' of the Christian Faith were not left to be discovered by man as circumstance or genius dictated. They were provided by God, *from outside* at a given time and place. However closely the subjective *discovery* of religious truth may be parallel to that of the physical sciences, sooner or later this fundamental cleavage is bound to appear, and it is a source of two-fold offence to the modern mind.

There is first what has been called " the stumbling-block of particularity ".[1] It is a common modern assumption that truth exists for all time, waiting only on the genius of the human discoverer to reveal it ; that if we go on long enough and search diligently enough we shall know all that there is to be known about everything. To claim that the truth of God, sufficient for the purposes of this mortal life, has been finally and irrevocably revealed by God himself in an age that is now long past, and highly unscientific withal, does not invite sympathetic consideration.

Secondly, there is the difficulty of adjustment to the idea of the supernatural. The attitude which says in effect, " If I cannot understand this, it can't be true " (an attitude frequently adopted towards the truths of religion), may be convenient in the laboratory, though even here it is false. For though we may tabulate and utilise the laws of chemistry or physics, we do not *understand* them. Towards religion such an attitude is fatal. If I, with my little mind, could comprehend God, I could not worship him, because God would then be no bigger than my mind, and I cannot worship the content of my own mind. Religion, since it is concerned with God, must contain an element of mystery. But the scientific-materialist temper revolts at mystery.

A still more serious problem for the Christian preacher is the fact that not only the technical terms of religion but

[1] Cf. J. S. Whale, *Christian Doctrine*, p. 62.

human language as a whole is ceasing to have its proper significance for our generation. As a result of modern national and political propaganda, words are rapidly losing their meaning. Every day in Europe the most blatant lies are broadcast in solemn oratory. One day we are told, " France will never be beaten ". The next day her capitulation is announced in equally high-sounding and plausible phrases. After four years of this daily rhetorical juggling very many words are ceasing to have any intellectual significance, and are used merely to stimulate the emotions, or to prevent the real truth from being realised (cf. ' target ', ' objective ', ' success ', etc.). Intelligent men are becoming distrustful of words, the masses are hypnotised by them. If the evangelist had to rely solely on the use of the spoken word, the success of his preaching would be, humanly speaking, precarious in the extreme.

Mercifully, the preaching of the Gospel is not entirely dependant on the use of language. It has been said that there is more converting power in one holy life than in hundreds of eloquent sermons. There is undoubtedly a truth here. But it does not render the spoken word unnecessary. In the last resort it is not possible to " spread the Gospel without preaching it ". However compelling may be the attractive power of the holy life, there is still a need for the word of interpretation which explains that life, and links it with the Christ who is its source.

There is also to be taken into account the fact that the life of no single Christian, however sanctified, can ever fully represent Christ. Hence the need for the witness of the community. The Gospel can never properly be preached apart from its context in the Christian Church.

The modern evangelist needs, therefore, some ways of presenting Christian truth which will meet some, if not all, of the difficulties outlined above. Though he will have to make use of the spoken word, he will realise its limitations, and will not depend on it entirely. His purpose is not only to meet the rationalising and materialist mind on its own ground, but to *get underneath* it; to kindle the imagination and to stimulate the will; to present the reality of the Christian Faith in a way that is reasonable yet not rationalistic, concrete yet not devoid of mystery, objective yet claiming personal allegiance. The method outlined in the foregoing chapters fulfils some, but not all, of these conditions. Its effectiveness must depend partly on the leader and the degree to which he is able to 'get across' to his hearers, and partly on the quality of the Christian group into which the 'hearers' or catechumens are introduced. As has already been said, apart from the spoken word of the preacher, the liturgy is the Church's other great medium of presenting her Gospel. The problem is to carry people sufficiently far in the Christian Faith to enable them to take an intelligent and worshipful part in the liturgy. There are two approaches to the mainsprings of human action, both of which have their place in liturgy, and both of which have been used by the Church apart from corporate worship. They are (1) Drama, and (2) Symbolism.

During the last few years there has been a vigorous revival of religious drama. Dramatic representations of our Lord's Passion and Resurrection were enacted early in Christian history. The first stages seem to have consisted in such simple ceremonies as the carrying of palms on Palm Sunday, and (later) the burying of the crucifix on Good Friday and its subsequent production on Easter Day. In time, however, such simple actions developed into real drama, introducing some of the characters and dialogue, based on the Biblical narratives of the great events of our Lord's life, death and resurrection. In mediæval England the mystery and miracle plays were one of the main vehicles of popular religious education, and the revival of some of these old plays has enabled us to realise their tremendously worshipful qualities. As Miss Dorothy Sayers has reminded us, " The Dogma is the Drama ", and the reverent presentation of the dogma-drama will often succeed where argument fails. It speaks to elements in the personality untouched by the sermon or the discussion-group.

> " Because the Gospel drama really happened, and is a racial experience, it can affect the minds that receive it at deeper as well as higher levels of consciousness than the intellectual, it may influence levels at which we dream. No other biography, history, social drama (for it is all these) has exerted through the imagination of men so strong a shaping force upon their world." [1]

Here, then, is an evangelistic medium of tremendous potentiality. That it needs skilful and sympathetic handling goes without saying. Especially should eager young clerics who have not seriously studied the dramatic art be discouraged from attempting to write their own nativity and Passion plays. There are available many good religious plays well within the scope of the personnel of the average parish, and it is safer to rely on the work of the competent craftsman than to indulge in amateur experiments which may or may not ' come off '.[2]

Our immediate concern is the relation between drama and worship. Generally speaking, religious drama as such, performed on the stage or in church, is a truth-teaching and a ' will-moving ' rather than a worship-training medium. The extent to which a religious play reverently and effectively presented may stimulate an attitude of worship will depend partly on the play itself and partly on the way in which it is produced. Where these are of the kind likely to give rise to spontaneous worship, opportunity can be given at the end

[1] Philip Mairet, *Christian News-Letter Supplement*, No. 126.
[2] Cf. *The Production of Religious Plays*, by E. Martin Browne. (S.P.C.K.)

of the play, but should consist largely of silence. Just as the effect of a good story can be ruined by pointing the moral after it has been told, so a good play should be left to tell its own tale. To preach a sermonette at the end is fatal. Similarly, to invite the congregation to sing a hymn at the conclusion of the performance is to run a grave risk of destroying the effect of the play. It switches people's minds away from the play on to the hymn, the tune of which will probably introduce wholly fresh and often alien associations. A brief bidding, a period of silence and one carefully chosen prayer are sufficient.

It is, however, possible to incorporate dramatic presentation into a liturgical action, so that the drama is used as a stimulus to an act of worship. The priest-in-charge of a seaside church recently tried a very successful experiment on these lines during the Sunday evenings of Lent. Instead of a sermon at Evensong, he used lantern-slides of the Oberammergau Passion Play and choral-speaking to supply the dramatic element which formed the introduction to a conducted meditation. The church can be quickly blacked out, so Evensong was sung in daylight. The screen was rolled up on the ground at the chancel steps, with ropes and pulleys ready fixed. During the hymn after the Third Collect the choir moved into the front seats of the nave, the screen was hauled into position, and sidesmen blacked out the windows. A little group of six picked choir-boys went to the piano (well out of sight), and a speaking-choir of three men and two young women took up their positions behind the screen. (The dim light they needed for reading was not sufficient to interfere with the illumination of the screen.)

On the first evening the priest gave an introductory talk, pointing out that there are more ways of praying than by kneeling down and saying words. He explained that the intention was to use the screen as a background for meditating upon the Passion of our Lord. He also said a few words about the Oberammergau Passion Play, the players in which certainly did not intend their performance to be regarded as mere entertainment. Each scene in that play was prefaced by an Old Testament tableau, put there to draw out the meaning and significance of our Lord's sufferings and death. During this meditation in church these Old Testament tableaux would be accompanied by choral speaking from behind the screen. For the slides giving the actual events of the Passion, the narrative would be read in the words of Holy Scripture from the back of the church. (This arrangement made it possible not only to mark the contrast between the Old and New Testament passages, so that no one could be puzzled by their juxtaposition, but also enabled the reader to be near the lantern and ensure that the slides were changed at exactly the right moment.) After the introduction, the people knelt and said the *Veni Creator*. They then sat, and the first slide was thrown upon the screen. It was the tableau of the expulsion of Adam and Eve from Eden. The chorus at once came in as follows :

Chorus. Adam and Eve have sinned.

    1st Girl's voice. The Lord God said unto Adam

    1st Man's voice. Hast thou eaten of the tree, whereof I commanded thee that thou shouldest not eat ?

    1st Girl's voice. And the man said

    2nd Man's voice. The woman whom thou gavest to be with me, she gave me of the tree, and I did eat.

    1st Girl's voice. And the Lord God said unto the woman

    1st Man's voice. What is this that thou hast done ?

    1st Girl's voice. And the woman said

    2nd Girl's voice. The serpent beguiled me and I did eat.

K

1st Girl's voice.   And the Lord God said

1st Man's voice.   Behold, the man is become as one of us to know good and evil.

1st Girl's voice.   Therefore the Lord God sent him forth from the garden of Eden to till the ground from whence he was taken.

So he drove out the man ; and placed at the east end of the garden of Eden Cherubim, and a flaming sword which turned every way, to keep the way of the tree of life.

Chorus.   Adam and Eve have sinned.   They are driven out from their happiness.

1st Girl's voice.   Until the second Adam comes

Chorus.   Who on the Cross will set man free from sin.

The slide then changed to ' Christ enters Jerusalem ', and the narrative, in the words of the New Testament, was read by the priest, slowly and without too much expression, so that the picture and the Gospel words might speak for themselves.   For some slides comment was given in music. For example, at our Lord's parting from his Mother the choir sang " Virgin-born, we bow before thee ", and, on later occasions, " My God, my God, and can it be ", " There is a green hill ", " He was despised ", etc.   Where necessary, the title of the New Testament slide was announced by a girl's voice.   On each evening there was one hymn slide near the middle of the meditation, which the whole congregation sang kneeling.   For instance, after the crucifixion slides they sang, as a prayer, " My God, I love thee ".   At the end of the meditation there were more conducted prayers, sometimes said by the congregation from the screen, sometimes read by the priest while suitable slides were thrown on the screen.   On the last evening, while the people knelt, the choir sang three verses of " O sacred Head ", while three of the most impressive slides were shown.

. The people came to these services in very considerable numbers. Some, no doubt, came from curiosity. But after the first few minutes the atmosphere was definitely that of worship.

The priest who conducted the experiment adds the following details, which may be of use to anyone who desires to make a similar venture.

" The slides used were those of the 1934 Oberammergau Passion Play, coloured. They were hired from Messrs. Newtons, in three sections, for two guineas. They were of exceptional standard, and the colouring was very beautiful. The experiment would necessarily have failed had not the best possible slides been used. The text used for the New Testament slides was collated from the four Gospels, in order to include, for example, all the seven words from the Cross. Where there was little in Holy Scripture to describe the scene portrayed, appropriate sayings of our Lord were used. Some of the tableaux were omitted either because the slide lacked clarity, or because the subject was too obscure. The chorus needs careful rehearsal. If the words cannot be learnt by heart, the members should practise taking their time from the leader's lips. Care must be taken to see that everything goes smoothly (e.g., no upside down slides !) The prayers, too, need careful preparation, if the performance is not to become an entertainment."

This experiment, though having the practical advantage of involving less preparation and rehearsing than the production of a staged religious drama, is in essence a dramatic method, since, like the drama, it makes use of a pictorial presentation of Biblical history together with the enunciation of the appropriate words. Its value for our purpose is that it appeals to more elemental and less critical, sophisticated levels of mind than does the reasoned presentation of religious truth in lectures and sermons. A child cannot think in words until he has acquired a moderate vocabulary, but he can and does think in concrete images of the people and things that make up his environment. The pictorial method of presentation, therefore, speaks directly to less conscious and rationalising levels of mind than do words.

This fact suggests yet another method of approach. Psychologists tell us that not only does the unconscious mind think in pictures, but also that the analysis of dreams reveals that certain pictures or images tend in the unconscious minds of different people to represent the same things. The images are called symbols. A symbol may be defined as an image which has a fairly uniform meaning for different people. The power of the symbol in ordinary life is too well known to need further description; witness the Union Jack, the Stars and Stripes and the Swastika, to take but the most obvious examples. The Christian religion has a symbolism of its own, the value of which both as a means of impression and also a vehicle of expression it would be foolish to ignore.

One symbol of elemental type and tremendous power is that of light. No one who has seen, for instance, the Toc H 'Ceremony of Light' can doubt that the significance of this symbol has not diminished because men have become more sophisticated than former generations. It is not surprising that quite early in Christian history the symbolic use of lighted candles should become attached to the sacrament of Baptism, and later find expression in such ceremonies as Candlemass, the use of altar lights and in a variety of ceremonies now common in many parts of the Church overseas. The following account (quoted from the Rev.

H. P. Thompson's *Worship in Other Lands* [1]) will serve to show the tremendous teaching power of some of these dramatic uses of the symbol of light.

"A very striking ' Festival of Lights ', missionary in its teaching, is held at Epiphany in the church of the American Church Mission at Hankow, and in some other churches. The service begins after sunset ; choir, clergy and congregation are seated in their usual places ; all lights are then extinguished. In the dark an address is given on the pitiable condition of those who ' sit in darkness and the shadow of death,' and the need of the world that does not know the true light. Still in the dark a hymn is sung, such as ' Christ whose glory fills the skies '. Then the ' Christ light ' is lit, a single candle set in the centre of the altar. Another brief address is given, recalling how few at first knew of Christ when he came to be the Light of the world : but others were in time to know it too, and men from afar were to come seeking it. Then by the light of the one candle the priest reads the gospel of the Epiphany. Then a well-known hymn is sung, ' Brightest and best are the sons of the morning ' ; and as it ends the three Wise Men move slowly forward from the back of the church, bearing real gold, frankincense and myrrh. They are three tall boys vested in copes and wearing gilt crowns. Each lays his gift on the altar, singing his verse from ' We three Kings of Orient are ', and the congregation joins in the refrain. Each king bears a taper and lights this from the Christ light on the altar : then turning to the congregation they light the tapers which all carry and the light is passed from one to another ; many candles on the altar are also set alight.

[1] H. P. Thompson, *Worship in Other Lands* (S.P.G.), pp. 101–103.

A brief address is given on the symbolism of spreading the light; the people are reminded of the darkness of heathenism outside the Church; and with incense and lights a procession is formed, which passes through the main door, singing Epiphany and missionary hymns, and carries the light into the darkness without.

"After returning to church solemn Evening is sung, as a thanksgiving for the Light of Christ, and an offering for missions is presented. At the end the people carry their lighted candles home through the dark streets—a fit symbol of the Christian's duty to spread the Light of Christ."

A similar use of the same symbol, though set in a rather different context, has for some years been enacted in a Norfolk village to celebrate the Feast of St. Andrew, the patron saint of ' Light-bearers '.

When the congregation is assembled, all the lights in the church are put out, and the service begins in complete darkness except for the light of the two altar candles. The Rector, who is in the pulpit, explains that these two candles symbolise the fact that our Lord Jesus Christ came to be the Light of the world, and describes how, on the day of Pentecost, the little band of disciples waiting in the upper room was empowered to spread the Light of Christ throughout the world. While he is speaking a figure can just be seen lighting a large standard candle set in front of the altar with a taper which he has kindled from the altar light. This, the Rector explains, represents the light of Pentecost, the light which the Church must spread. He then goes on to tell of how the first Apostles took the Church's light to the various parts of the Mediterranean world. Men, dressed to represent the apostles, then emerge from the choir-stalls, each bearing a candle, which he lights from ' the candle of the

Church ' and takes to some part of the chancel and places it in a previously prepared socket. The Rector then invites the congregation to join in prayer about the work of the apostles, after which an appropriate hymn is sung. The story is then continued from the pulpit, describing how St. Aidan and St. Augustine brought ' the Light ' to England. Men, dressed to represent these two saints, preceded by a crucifer, and each carrying his candle, kindled from one of the apostolic lights, then process from the chancel to the Lady-chapel, where they plant their candles. Another prayer period ensues, the subject-matter of the prayers being ' The conversion of England ', followed by a suitable hymn.

The next stage in the action concerns the parish. The Rector tells of how their first incumbent, Richard de Repps, in the twelfth century brought the Light to their own village. This is then enacted, candles are lit on the chancel screen, and the congregation joins in prayer for the parish. When the congregation has become seated again, the conductor explains how generations of people in their village have received the Light from the Font, and stresses the fact that they have each received the Light not only that it may guide them in their own lives, but that they may pass it on to others. He describes the people of other lands dwelling " in darkness and in the shadow of death ", and impresses his hearers with their missionary responsibility. This short address is the introduction to what is the most moving piece of drama in the service. Three tiny children, from the Infant Sunday School, come and light their candles from those on the Font, and without any adult prompting sing, " Jesus bids us shine, with a clear, pure light ". They then take their candles and set them in the Children's Corner. This completed, the ' people of the village ' come out from their pews, light their candles from the Font and take their candles and take them to sockets placed on the ledges of the windows in the nave. As the light shines out from these candles, pictures, fastened to the wall immediately underneath each window, become visible. The picture under one window is revealed as a scene in Central Africa, another depicts the people of China, another shows a village in India, and so on. There follows a time of prayer for the work of the Church overseas, and the service concludes with a procession of all the 'Light-bearers' who have taken part in it.

No one who has ever witnessed this service could ever forget it, nor is there any doubt that it is primarily what it sets out to be, an act of prayer and worship. The symbolism is simple and unmistakable. The action moves steadily forward from complete darkness (except for the twin points of light on the altar) to a blaze of light, hundreds of twinkling candles shedding their soft radiance over the church and congregation.

An ancient and dramatic use of the same symbol incorporated into the first Evensong of Christmas has been revived at Exeter Cathedral, where it was introduced by that most efficient prelate and learned liturgiologist, Bishop John De Grandisson (Bishop of Exeter, 1331–1369). After the first Lesson, a boy chorister, habited in alb and amice and carrying a lighted candle, comes from behind the High Altar, and taking his stand at the altar-step, announces to the people in the choir the good news of the Incarnation by singing, *Hodie nobis coelorum rex de virgine nasci dignatus est*.[1] While the choir take up and complete this respond, other lights are lit; the choir-boy moves westwards, and is joined first by six other boys, and then by two Priest-Vicars habited in copes. The choir then sing the *Gloria in excelsis deo*. The procession having come to the screen, the Priest-Vicars pass on the glad tidings to the people assembled in the nave, repeating

[1] "Today for us the King of Heaven hath deigned to be born of a virgin."

the *Hodie nobis*, to which the seven boys make appropriate response. The whole choir then sing a short anthem of praise while the procession returns, and Evensong is continued with the *Magnificat*.

It will be observed that this ceremony is a dramatisation of the account given by St. Luke, and makes use of two symbols—light and movement. As the news is carried from the High Altar to the congregation, so more and more lights are lit.

Ordered movement can itself be full of significance; witness the age-long use of the procession as an act of worship. An S.P.G. Festival Service which is in essence a piece of dramatic worship based on the principle underlying the procession has recently been used in St. Paul's Church, Bedford, and is reproduced in Appendix A.

These illustrations will suffice to show that in a wise use of the dramatic method there is an instrument of great potential value to those clergy and evangelists who are faced with the task of trying to teach the art of worship to people of this sophisticated generation. There is room for careful study of and experimentation in this medium. But heed should be paid to the warning and advice contained in the following letter from a Vicar who has had considerable experience in this field.

" With regard to liturgy as a quasi-dramatic form, the first essential is a thorough understanding of the rites and ceremonies of the Western Church. T. S. Eliot in his ' Dialogue on Dramatic Poetry ' (*Selected Essays* : 1932, p. 47) makes one of his characters say,

' The only dramatic satisfaction that I find now is in a High Mass well performed. Have you not there everything necessary ? And, indeed, if you

consider the ritual of the Church during the cycle
of the year, you have the complete drama represented. The Mass is a small drama, having all
the verities. But in the Church's year you have
represented the full drama of creation.'

In the Church year, with the traditional ceremonies as
still practised in the Church of Rome, you have the drama
of creation, the process of many centuries of development, a folk process if ever there was one, and instinct
with the quite unrivalled dramatic creativeness of the
Christian religion. In the three masses of Christmas,
the Holy Week ceremonies, Tenebrae, stripping of the
altar after the Maundy Thursday Mass, the blessing of
the first-fire, etc., the May-day processions, the litanies
in procession, the observances at a requiem with the
catafalque and candles—and as the main-pin of everything, the ceremonial of the High Mass itself, and the
reading of the Daily Offices; you have a body of
dramatic worship *which must be the norm*. I believe
that the Church of England ought to be quite drastic in
its handling of this tradition, as I will show later on.
But the first point is that there exists a norm which every
innovator should study before he sets about his work.
It is not only the words and ceremonies that so many
folk are ignorant of, it is the basic rules and principles
of personal behaviour. Liturgy is highly stylised and
impersonal. It is above all things the representation
in terms of words and ceremonial action of the saving
work of God in Christ ' until He come '. It is therefore
essentially doctrinal. Every ceremony has its core of
dogma. Any liturgical novelties that are entered upon
in ignorance of this body of tradition and in independence of these rules should be discouraged. There are

Bishops who, ' to make the thing more real ', adopt hearty or slovenly or personalist stances at the altar; priests who read *e.g.* the invitation to Communion and confession in a heart-broken voice. Ugh! When the priest puts on his priestly vestments (a ' dramatic ' adjunct of first-class importance) he puts on Christ. He is not the Rev. John Smith, but the priest. That is, his personality is stylised out of the way of the people's prayers. He should speak in a steady, impersonal voice, and use the traditional gestures. Again, one sees the urge to display and stimulate interest through the visual organs flowing out into the drum-head kind of service, with a lot of flag-wagging completely foreign to Catholic tradition and without any relevance to Christian doctrine. Ceremonies that are not *instinct with Christian doctrine are* awful, like the bowdlerised hymns in *Songs of Praise.*

" Because ceremonial is a traditional art, based on the events of the saving action of God, and instinct with Christian doctrine, it is not to be expected that everyone will understand it at once. Significance is not to be sacrificed to simplicity.

" On the other hand, Roman rite and ceremony are both, to some extent, distorted, and, in any case, we in the Church of England, and the mass of the people in the land, have lost contact. We are, in practice, starting *de noveau* to build up a liturgical practice, or rather, we are beginning with a few simple characteristics already formed, the elaboration of which will give us a tradition superior to that which prevails at present in most parts of the Church of Rome. The participation of the laity in the liturgy is axiomatic in Anglicanism, thank God. We have also a permanently bad conscience in the matter of over-elaboration of detail; we value the smooth and simple.   We are accustomed to the thought that churchgoing has an implication with regard to conduct. . . ." [1]

[1] The Rev. P. J. Lamb, Vicar of St. Aidan's, Leeds.

APPENDICES

A.

ORDER OF FESTIVAL SERVICE

NOTE OF EXPLANATION.—*This processional service is a symbolic act. The procession of clergy as it moves round the church is representative of the missionary action of the Church in the four quarters of the globe. It speaks also of the day's work, as the sun moves forward from dawn to dusk. The service is composed of five sections with sermon and conclusion. Each section, preceded by verses of a hymn, consists of an introduction, Bible reading, and prayer. In each case the congregation is asked to stand for the hymn and introduction, sit for the reading, and kneel for prayer. The procession moves first to the Nave and makes an act of penitence for the Home Church.*

HYMN E.H. 387 (Tune A. & M. 164).

THE DARK HOUR

Conductor:

"And the earth was without form and void, and darkness was upon the face of the deep."—Gen. i, 2.

"And when the sixth hour was come there was darkness over the whole earth until the ninth hour."—Mark xv, 33.

V. O Lord, deal not with us after our sins.

R. Neither reward us after our iniquities.

LET US PRAY

O God, merciful father, that despiseth not the sighing of a contrite heart, nor the desire of such as be sorrowful; mercifully assist our prayers that we make before thee in all our troubles and adversities whensoever they oppress us; and graciously hear us, that those evils, which the craft and subtlety of the devil or man worketh against us be brought to naught and by the providence of thy goodness they may be dispersed; that we, thy servants, being hurt by no persecutions, may evermore give thanks unto thee in thy holy Church, through Jesus Christ our Lord.—*Amen*.

R. O Lord, arise, help us and deliver us for thy Name's sake.

O God, we have heard with our ears and our fathers have declared unto us the noble works that thou didst in their days and in the old time before them.

R. O Lord, arise, help us and deliver us for thine honour.

Most gracious Father, we humbly beseech thee for thy holy Catholic Church. Fill it with all truth; in all truth with all peace. Where it is corrupt, purge it; where it is in error, direct it; where anything is amiss, reform it; where it is right, strengthen and confirm it; where it is in want, furnish it; where it is divided and rent asunder, make up the breaches of it, O thou Holy One of Israel.—*Amen*.

Space for Silent Prayer

THE DAWN

Reading:

" Jesus said: All power is given unto me in heaven and in earth. Go ye, therefore, and teach all nations, baptising them in the name of the Father and of the Son and of the Holy Ghost."— Matt. xxviii, 18.

" The Spirit of the Lord is upon me, because he hath anointed me to preach good tidings. And they shall build the old wastes. They shall raise up the former desolations and they shall repair the waste cities. Nation shall not lift up sword against nation, neither shall they learn war any more."—Isaiah lxi, 1.

LET US PRAY

Grant, O Lord, to thy Church in Europe that through thy abiding presence being made steadfast in tribulation and purified through suffering, she may show forth thy Word at this time with such power and love that the nations may be set free from every weakness and iniquity to serve thee in newness of life to the praise of thy Holy Name.—*Amen.*

V. Let us go forth in peace.

R. In the name of the Lord.—*Amen.*

HYMN 373 E.H., verses 1 and 2

The procession moves to the east and halts under the tower.

THE DAY'S WORK

EAST. IN THE MORNING

Conductor:

As we face the east, from whence comes the light, let us pray that Christ, the Son of Righteousness, may shine on all the world.

Reading:

"Arise, shine, for thy light is come, and the glory of the Lord is risen upon thee."—Isaiah lx, 1.

V. They shall come from the east and from the west, and from the north and from the south.

R. And shall sit down in the Kingdom of God.

Acts of Praise and Intercession:

Let us thank God for the Church of Jerusalem, the Mother of all Churches, and for James, the brother of our Lord, its first bishop.

Let us thank God for Peter and the holy band of the Apostles, going forth as missionaries from the Upper Room to found the Catholic Church throughout the world.

Let us pray for the peace of Jerusalem to-day, and for the solution of all difficulties in the Holy Land.

Let us pray for all who dwell in the Near East under the cloud of war, and for the reconciliation to the true faith of all Jews, Turks and Mohammedans.

Space for Silent Prayer.

Conductor :

Now let us lift up our eyes to the farther East.

Reading :

" Who are these that fly as a cloud, and as doves to their windows ? "—Isaiah lx, 8.

V.   Thy sons shall come from far.

R.   And thy daughters shall be nursed at thy side.

Acts of Praise and Intercession :

Let us thank God for the Church in India, and for the conversion of many to the Christian faith.

Let us thank God for the Church in China, in all her distresses, and for the constancy of her witness and the courage of her leaders.

Let us thank God for the Church in the Commonwealths of Australia and New Zealand, and for the good seed sown in the islands of the Pacific.

Let us pray for the Churches now separated from their brethren, in Japan and Korea, that they may remain steadfast in loyalty to their Lord.

Let us pray for the reunion of Christendom in God's good time.

Everlasting Father, the radiance of faithful souls, who didst bring nations to thy light, and kings to the brightness of thy rising, fill, we beseech thee, the world with thy glory, and show thyself unto all the nations ; through him who is the true light and the bright and morning star, Jesus Christ the Son, our Lord.— *Amen.*

HYMN 373, E.H., verses 3 and 4

The procession moves to the South Pulpit.

SOUTH. WORK AT MID-DAY

Conductor :

As we face the south let us remember that the Epistle is read towards the south, because in Apostolic days the newly-converted faithful lived in that quarter.

Reading :

"And the eunuch said : See, here is water. What doth hinder me from being baptised ? And Philip said : If thou believest with all thy heart, thou mayest. And he answered and said : I believe that Jesus Christ is the Son of God."—Acts viii, 36.

" Fear not, I am with thee. I will say to the north give up, and to the south keep not back. Bring my sons from far and my daughters from the ends of the earth. Let all nations be gathered together, and let all people be assembled. Let them hear and say : It is truth."—Isaiah xliii, 9.

V. Ye are my witnesses, saith the Lord.

R. That I am God.

Acts of Praise and Intercession :

Let us thank God for the great Church of Alexandria, for St. Mark and St. Athanasius, for the Church of Carthage and North Africa, and for St. Cyprian and St. Augustine of Hippo.

Let us thank God for the Gospel taken to darkest Africa by missionary saints and heroes in our own days.

Let us pray for the child races in Africa, that they may be brought up in the fear and nurture of the Lord, and to the praise of his Holy Name.

Let us pray for our fellow-countrymen in their special responsibility for the peace and progress of the African continent.

Let us pray for the Abyssinian Church and people in their newly-restored liberty.

Enlarge thy Kingdom, O God, and deliver the world from the dominion and tyranny of Satan. Hasten the time which thy spirit hath foretold, when all nations whom thou hast made shall come and worship thee and glorify thy Name. Bless the good

L

endeavours of those who strive to propagate the truth, and prepare the hearts of all in Africa to receive it, to the honour of thy name, through Jesus Christ our Lord.—*Amen.*

HYMN 466 E.H., verses 1 and 2

The procession moves to the west.

WEST.   WORK AFTER NOON

Conductor :

As we face the west let us thank God for the enlargement of man's opportunity by the discovery of the New World.

Reading :

" The Lord thy God will make thee plenteous in every work of thine, in the fruit of thy body, in the fruit of thy cattle, in the fruit of thy land, if thou shalt hearken unto the voice of the Lord thy God, to keep his commandments.   For this commandment is not hidden from thee, neither is it far off.   It is not in heaven, that thou shouldest say, Who shall go up for us to heaven, and bring it unto us, that we may hear it, and do it ?   Neither is it beyond the seas, that thou shall say, Who shall go over the sea for us and bring it unto us ?   But the word is very nigh unto thee ; in thy mouth and in thy heart that thou mayest do it."—Deut. xxx, 11.

V.   For from the rising of the sun even unto the going down of the same my Name shall be great among the Gentiles.

R.   And in every place incense shall be offered unto my Name, and a pure offering.

Acts of Praise and Intercession :

Let us pray for our brethren beneath the western sky.

Let us thank God that the Society for the Propagation of the Gospel, first formed to supply the religious needs of settlers, has grown at length to cover the earth.

Let us thank God for the Church in the United States, and for her splendid generosity shown at this time to Church of England Missionary Societies.

Let us thank God for the Church in Canada, for its missionary zeal, and for its enterprise in meeting the needs of lonely settlers, and for its support for the Home Church in her hour of need.

Let us pray for the Church in the West Indies, and that a special blessing may rest upon her work among women.

O Lord, without whom our labour is but lost, and with whom the weakest go forth as mighty; be present to all works in thy Church which are undertaken according to thy will, especially in the lands of North and South America, and grant to thy labourers a pure intention, patient faith, sufficient success upon earth, and the bliss of serving thee in heaven; through Jesus Christ our Lord.— *Amen.*

Hymn 466 E.H., verses 3 and 6

The procession moves to the north.

North. Work at Eventide

Conductor:

We face the north. It is towards the north that the Gospel is read at the Holy Eucharist, to remind us that to the first Christians our lands were still the heathen north to which the Gospel had to be preached.

Reading:

"And the Lord said unto Abram: Lift up now thine eyes and look from the place where thou art, northward and southward, and eastward and westward. For all the land which thou seest, to thee will I give it and thy seed for ever. Then Abram removed his tent and built there an altar unto the Lord."—Gen. xiii. 14.

V. Praise the Lord upon earth, ye dragons and all deeps.

R. Fire and hail, snow and vapours, wind and storm fulfilling his word.

Acts of Praise and Intercession :

Let us thank God for the coming of the Gospel in Roman times to our island, sunk in heathen darkness.

Let us thank God for Alban, the first Christian martyr in Britain, the patron saint of this our Diocese, and for all saints and missionaries who came to our shores.

Let us thank God for the revival of missionary zeal at long last in the eighteenth century.

Let us pray for the Diocese in the Arctic, for the Church in Scandinavia, for the Church in Russia, and for all whose work for Christ brings them in peril of body or mind.

Let us pray for all who sail the icy seas, as fishermen, merchant seamen, or as men of the King's navy ; for garrison troops in northern lands, in the hardships and perils of war.

Assist us mercifully, O Lord, in these our supplications and prayers, and dispose the way of thy servants towards the attainment of everlasting salvation, that among all the changes and chances of this mortal life, they may ever be defended by thy most gracious and ready help ; through Jesus Christ our Lord.—*Amen.*

Hymn 545 E.H.

During the singing of this hymn the procession moves to the Choir.

THE SERMON

Hymn 535, E.H., Pt. I.

The Bishop proceeding to the High Altar, and the procession halting before him in a twelve-unit square, the Bishop shall then say :

"And he carried me away in the spirit to a great and high mountain, and showed me that great city, the holy Jerusalem, descending out of heaven from God—on the east three gates, on the north three gates, on the south three gates, and on the west three gates. And the walls of the city were twelve pearls. And the city lieth four-square. And they shall bring the glory and the honour of the nations into it."—Rev. xxi, 10.

V. And he saith unto me : These sayings are true and faithful. Behold, I come quickly.

R. *Amen.* Even so come, Lord Jesus.

THE LORD'S PRAYER

THE BLESSING

HELPS AND HINDRANCES TO INTELLIGENT WORSHIP

IF we hope to persuade some of those who are at present non-church-goers that the corporate worship of God is not only a privilege but a duty, and also that the Church's liturgical worship is worth taking trouble to appreciate and intelligently to share, it follows that our normal method of handling our services in church must be such as to strengthen, and not to weaken this conviction. Unfortunately this is not always the case. There are many usages common in our churches which do not make for an intelligent understanding of liturgy, and which, indeed, are not calculated to convince the initiate in the art of worship that we possess much common, let alone liturgical, sense. I am not here referring to the use or misuse of the traditional ceremonies of the altar nor to liturgical minutiæ about which only competent liturgiologists can speak with authority, but to the more obvious exhibitions of misunderstanding or gaucherie which are frequently perpetrated during the Sunday rendering of the Choir offices. Of these the following seem to call for comment.

Opening and Closing.

The most glaring example of thoughtless liturgical iconoclasm is the addition of ' opening ' and ' closing ' hymns to Sunday Mattins and Evensong. The practice of adding hymns, a sermon and a blessing to the Sunday office is so well established that it does not occur to many people that these things are additions at all. The usage is, however, one for which as an expression of popular devotion there is considerable justification. But for the custom of adding further ' opening ' and ' closing ' ceremonies there is no justification whatever. Morning and Evening Prayer begin on a note of penitence ; then follows praise, introduced by " O Lord, open thou our lips ".[1] If the congregation is invited to begin by

[1] Or, as some would express it, Morning and Evening Prayer have a penitential *introduction*, the service proper beginning with

singing a hymn (either by way of covering the movement of the choir from the vestry to the chancel, or after the choir and clergy have taken up their positions therein), not only is the subsequent " O Lord, open thou our lips " rendered absurd, but the whole movement and balance of the service have been spoiled. Many clergy who continue the practice are uncomfortably aware of this, but retain it because " the people like it ". They only like it because some past vicar, who ought to have known better, taught them to like it. They should now be taught that in Mattins and Evensong praise is meant to follow penitence—and why.

Similarly, the service should end with the Blessing. To add a vesper hymn or a ' recessional ' (or both !) is to create an anti-climax. Nor is it in the least necessary that the congregation should hear the choir's vestry prayer, still less that it should be sung by the priest before he enters the vestry and that the choir should respond with a sung "Amen " calculated to penetrate into the farthest recesses of the church.

Incidentally, at the beginning of the service, what is the point of the choir and clergy kneeling for an uncomfortable and unreal two minutes immediately after taking their places in the chancel, when they have had their preparatory prayer in the vestry ? Surely the most seemly and logical procedure is for the choristers to enter quietly from the vestry, take up their places in the choir-stalls, and then for the service to begin. As the Prayer Book does not specify the posture to be taken up by the congregation during the sentence and exhortation, there is something to be said for the following order. At the entry of the choir and clergy the congregation stands, and remain standing until the former are in their stalls. Then all kneel and remain kneeling during the sentence and brief exhortation to confession and absolution (except, of course, the priest, who stands for the declaration of forgiveness) until the *Gloria*.

" O Lord, open thou our lips ". Cf. Procter and Frere, p. 373 ; " The old traditional musical use confirms this real structural division, but of late years a bad custom has arisen of beginning the singing and monotone before the versicle *O Lord, open thou our lips* ; this not only obscures the structural division but is in itself ridiculously out of harmony with the general meaning of the words."

After the Blessing at the conclusion of the service the choir should return quietly to the vestry, and the door shut, so that any further prayers that are said there are not audible to the congregation.

Hymns

Those who favour the use of ' opening ' and ' closing ' hymns may be disinclined to curtail them on the ground that the people like singing hymns, and that hymns are a useful expression of popular devotion.   One suspects that the popularity frequently surpasses the devotion, but in any case, there are by common custom three hymns still left, and these ought to suffice.   When full allowance has been made for the undoubted value of good hymns, and their place in the affections of worshipping people, it is nevertheless true that to sing more than three hymns at Mattins or Evensong is seriously to interfere with the logic and balance of the service.   The thoughtless multiplication of hymns tends to give them a prominence out of all proportion to their liturgical importance or their devotional value.   Though the subject of hymnology is pregnant with the possibilities of airing one's personal preferences (and to that extent it is a subject about which people may legitimately disagree), yet in the interests of intelligent worship there are some things which ought to be said. (Let those disagree who will.)

Many of the hymns in our hymn-books are more suited to personal prayer than to corporate worship.   Expressions of intense personal devotion do not always fit well into a liturgical setting, and should be used sparingly.   Many other hymns, not least some of those that are popular, stand condemned by reason of their theology, their language or their music, or by all three. Congregations are usually conservative in the matter of hymns, and the raising of the standard of hymnody in a particular church may seem a formidable task.   Yet if worship is to be significant and intelligent it must often be attempted.   Especially is this true in the case of hymn tunes.   The tune to which a hymn is sung often leaves a deeper impression on the mind than the words to which it is set.   Hence the need for ensuring that the impression left is a right one. How many people have an entirely false idea of the Christian religion because it is associated in their minds with cheap, sentimental, soporific hymn-tunes ? It is useless to try to teach people to value the beauty, dignity and objectivity of the liturgy if when they come to church they are assailed by sugary and maudlin music. Bad art is never good religion, and it is surely part of a parson's job to know what constitutes a good, and what a bad hymn tune.

A further factor to be considered is the relation of the music to the words of a hymn. Not only should the tune be suited to and expressive of the words ; it must not dominate them. Some hymns are popular simply because people like the tune. It would matter little if the words were in an unknown tongue. I once heard the hymn ' Glorious things of thee are spoken ' sung to the air of the great triumphal chorus in Beethoven's Ninth Symphony. Apart from the musical vandalism involved, it was grossly unfair to the hymn. Who is going to bother about the words and what they mean with such a powerful, dominating tune as that ? The air was everything, the words nothing. Compare the tunes ' Down Ampney ' (E.H. 152) and ' Gwalch-mai ' (E.H. 424), which so exactly express the sentiment of the hymns to which they are set that it is almost impossible to think of either tune without thinking of them in terms of the words. It is better that the tune should be subordinate to the words than that it should dominate them.

In this connection a word should be said about Plainsong. It is not necessary to be a plainsong enthusiast to realise that from the point of view of worship and devotion there is much to be said for *some* plainsong. The attitude which would exclude it altogether is surely as unenlightened as that which will tolerate nothing else. In passing, it is relevant to remember that " that increasingly rare bird, the man-in-the-pew " is unable to join in the singing of many of our hymns because the pitch is too high for his voice. A judicious use of plainsong, being more within his compass, would give him the opportunity to sing at least some of the service.

Many churches still favour a pointless and distracting ritual in the matter of announcing hymns; "Hymn number two hundred and forty-two, ' We love the place, O God '. The two hundred and forty-second hymn." Why all this fuss? Why, indeed, should hymns be announced at all? Most churches have hymn-boards a-plenty. Let the numbers of the hymns be clearly displayed thereon, and let each hymn be announced by the playing of the first two or three bars on the organ. Everything should be done to secure the minimum of interference with the smooth flow of the service.

Thoughtless and Meaningless Practices

The desire to appeal and to please has during recent years given rise to the introduction of several strange customs which might well be re-examined by the standards of liturgical significance and good taste. The presentation of the colours of the local Scout troop, Guide company or Cadet corps is harmless enough, and doubtless delights not a few. But when the incumbent stands in front of the altar with each colour, and solemnly makes the sign of the cross with the flag held vertically before his face, one begins to wonder what it is all about. The multiplication of ceremonies that are not "instinct with Christian doctrine" should be watched and discouraged.

The taking and presentation of alms is another ceremony calling for a little more clear thought than is often given to it. The proper place for the formal and ceremonial presentation of the people's offerings is, of course, the Eucharist. But there seems to be no good reason why the alms given at Mattins and Evensong should not also be presented at the altar, as the 1928 rubric allows, provided that the amount of ceremony used for the purpose is not allowed to become disproportionate to its importance in the service. To throw the presentation of alms into greater pro-minence at Mattins and Evensong than at the Eucharist, of which it is an integral and important part, is obviously misguided. Similarly, for the alms-dish solemnly to be carried out by the priest (as if it contained his spoils!) or the churchwarden is not in the best taste, to say the least of it. It is better to leave the alms in the sanctuary, from whence they may be quietly removed to the vestry after the service.

The Blessing

The desire to please has prompted some clergy to reduce the Blessing to a pious wish by the inclusion of the absent. "All those near and dear to you" have probably been prayed for earlier, but in any case they cannot be blessed if they are not physically present. The Blessing is a priestly and liturgical act, not to be confused with the offering of a prayer. A prayer can, of course, be substituted for a blessing at the end of Mattins and Evensong, and any absent from church can then be included in it. But such a prayer should not be said facing the congregation.[1]

Large Buildings

Our church buildings, beautiful though many of them are, can frequently be a great handicap because of their great size, especially in the country, where congregations tend to be disproportionately small in relation to the vastness of the church. When, as often happens, members of the congregation insist on sitting as far away from one another as possible, there is a loss of relationship between one worshipper and another, and between minister and congregation. All corporate sense is lost, and the preacher can never be *en rapport* with his hearers. The physical distance is too great. For corporate mental and spiritual activity physical proximity is extremely important, and all possible steps should be taken to ensure that people and priest are not separated by wide open spaces, even if it means roping off some rear portions of the church, and making one's peace with Mrs. Smith, who has sat in that particular pew for twenty years.

A similar difficulty arises at the Eucharist, where there is a long chancel containing empty choir-stalls separating the celebrant from the people. The priest is too far away from the worshippers

[1] On the principle laid down by the Bishops at the Savoy Conference that when the minister "speaks to the people (as in Lessons Absolution and Benedictions) it is convenient that he turn to them. When he speaks for them to God, it is fit that they should all turn another way."

for them to have a real part in what he is doing at the altar.   Many an attempt to establish the Parish Communion in the affections of the people has been wrecked on no more serious ground than this, and no one has quite realised what has been wrong !   The solution would appear to be the use of a portable nave-altar, so that celebrant and people can be nearer together.   In many a country church chairs could be put in the chancel for the early celebration on Sundays.   On weekdays a side chapel would naturally be used.

Similarly, many clergy have discovered the great psychological advantage of being amongst their people in the now widespread practice of leading the second set of prayers at Evensong from the middle of the nave aisle.   This custom has an additional advantage in the suggestion conveyed by the fact that priest and people face the same way.

C.

CHURCH PARADES AND SPECIAL SERVICES

1. *Church Parade Services*

During war-time the desire of various uniformed bodies to attend 'Church Parades', and the multiplication of special occasions that involve the presence in church of many non-churchgoers, present to the clergy a special form of the problem to which the foregoing chapters are devoted, and to which the principles they describe apply with special force. When a unit of one of the armed forces or of a local pre-service training corps asks the Vicar for a Church Parade, what is he to do? Much, of course, will depend on the occasion and on the proportion of regular worshippers (Anglican and non-Anglican) involved. In most cases, it is safe to assume that there are many in the unit who are ignorant of the Christian Faith, and unaccustomed to Christian worship. Sometimes the motives that prompt such parades are distinctly questionable (a desire to clothe the organisation with the garment of religious respectability or to attract public attention for purposes of recruiting). But except in cases where the motive is blatantly and admittedly unworthy,[1] there are few clergy who will not see in such parades an evangelistic opportunity to be accepted and used.

Broadly speaking, there are two types of Church Parade:

1. That at which, for reasons of convenience or suitability, the unit attends as a body one of the ordinary Sunday services of the church.

2. That which involves a separate and special service.

Where the parade is of the first type, and embraces people who are used to a different kind of worship or none at all, the priest responsible will naturally be careful to seek opportunity to explain the service sometime *before* the Sunday. Experience

---

[1] In such cases the best course may be to ask whether it would not be more appropriate to hold the parade in the open air, or in some building other than the church.

has shown that such informal preparatory instructions are both welcome and valuable. It need hardly be said that when strangers are present at one of the normal church services, the spiritual quality of the worship of the ordinary members of the congregation is a factor of considerable importance.

Where the uniformed body has a special service, the priest is presented with an excellent opportunity, but an opportunity that can be completely thrown away by the hotch-potch of hackneyed hymns together with bits of Mattins followed by an address which is not infrequently provided on such occasions.

As it is likely that Church Parades of one kind or another will continue after the war, and in view of the growth of workshop and other similar 'services', it is worth giving some thought to the perfection of a technique calculated to make the best possible use of the opportunities for teaching and training that they afford.

The underlying principle (see Chapter III) is that the worshippers should be invited to join in the appropriate acts of devotion *after* their minds have been stimulated and prepared by the address. The plan of the service will therefore be roughly as follows :

1. BRIEF ACT OF RECOLLECTION (with or without a hymn).
2. ADDRESS. This will usually deal with some basic truth or aspect of the Christian Faith, and will lead directly into—
3. THE ACT(S) of prayer, praise, confession or thanksgiving suitable to the occasion or the address. Here use will be made of silence, versicles and responses and spoken prayers. Often this period will be summed up in some liturgical prayer or thanksgiving, said (or sung) by the whole congregation (as described on pp. 78–83).
4. HYMN and BLESSING.

The above outline represents a framework, into which considerable variety of content will be introduced. Versicles and responses will be chosen to suit the purpose of the silent devotion to which they are designed to give expression. A lesson will sometimes be read before, or after, or even in the course of the address. A hymn may frequently be used as a prayer. In cases where a regular parade attended by the same people is held, the conductor will be able to plan his teaching and worship-training in a consecutive syllabus, thus leading his congregation step by step into richer fields of faith and worship. His form of service will gradually be amended accordingly.

2. *Special Occasions*

In many parishes there occur during the year certain special occasions which, though they do not belong exclusively or at all to the worshipping congregation, yet render appropriate a public recognition of God. For such occasions [1] (*e.g.*, the birthday of a local school or the annual festival of some laudable organisation) involving people who are at vastly different levels of Christian faith and of different Christian traditions, or even of none, the Prayer Book services are clearly unsuitable. They were not designed for such purposes, and it is not, in such cases, the Church *qua* Church which is at worship. Some special form of service must therefore be drawn up, and it may be worth while to consider the principles which should guide its construction.

1. The address should immediately *precede* the central ' act ' of the occasion, in order that the people's minds may be prepared for the thanksgiving or re-dedication or whatever is the main purpose of the gathering.

2. It is a wise practice to begin with a brief bidding which explains the purpose of the service and leads into an act of preparatory recollection.

3. If the members of the assembly are to join in such vocal parts in the service as are assigned to them, with promptitude and freedom from uncertainty about ' what is going to happen next ', they should be provided with a printed form of service. Unfortunately, however, the use of a printed form, though an aid to uniformity of bodily and

---

[1] I am not, of course, referring to national occasions for which a printed form of service is issued by authority ; still less to ' Farm Sunday ' and similar attempts to displace the Church's Calendar by celebrations of a national or even purely secular character. I refer to *local* occasions which involve no compromise of the Church's standards of worship or alteration of her services.

vocal activity, is, for most people, not conducive to a similar activity of mind and spirit. When it comes to prayer, the printed word tends to be a hindrance rather than a help.

It is a wise plan, therefore, to effect a compromise by printing the introductory part of the service in full, and the remainder in outline, providing only such responses or prayers as the congregation is required to say aloud. By this arrangement it is easy for the conductor, immediately after his address, to tell the people what he wants them to do with their *minds* in the prayer-time, and they are free from the distraction of the printed page.

The following skeleton will illustrate these suggestions:

FORM OF SERVICE

BIDDING

Brethren, we have come together, etc. . . . Let us therefore remember the God in whose Name we have met.

ACT OF FAITH AND WORSHIP

V. The heavens declare the glory of God.
R. The firmament sheweth his handiwork.

V. Be ye sure that the Lord, he is God.
R. It is he that hath made us and not we ourselves.

V. Of old it was said " No man hath seen God at any time ".
R. Jesus said, " He that hath seen me, hath seen the Father ".

V. By this we know that we dwell in him and he in us.
R. Because he hath given us of his Spirit.

V. Give the Lord the honour due unto His Name.
R. Worship the Lord with holy worship.

V. Let us come before his presence with thanksgiving.
R. And shew ourselves glad in him with psalms.

PSALM or HYMN
SCRIPTURE READING
HYMN

ADDRESS

ACT OF THANKSGIVING (or Re-dedication, etc.).

After each of the several Thanksgivings:

The Minister will say: *For Jesus Christ's sake.*
And the People will reply: *We thank thee, O God.*

Minister: Let us gather all our thanksgivings together, and say:

People: Almighty God, Father of all mercies, we thine unworthy servants do give thee most humble and hearty thanks for all thy goodness and loving-kindness to us and to all men. We bless thee for our creation, preservation, and all the blessings of this life; but above all for thine inestimable love in the redemption of the world by our Lord Jesus Christ, for the means of grace, and for the hope of glory. And we beseech thee, give us that due sense of all thy mercies, that our hearts may be unfeignedly thankful, and that we shew forth thy praise, not only with our lips, but in our lives; by giving up ourselves to thy service, and by walking before thee in holiness and righteousness all our days; through Jesus Christ our Lord, to whom with thee and the Holy Ghost be all honour and glory, world without end.—*Amen.*

The Lord's Prayer.

The Grace.

HYMN

BLESSING

The nature of the 'Act' after the address will naturally be determined by the occasion. It may also be wise to insert an 'Act' of some other type of devotion before the address, *e.g.*, to have an Act of Thanksgiving before the address, and the Act of Re-dedication after it. The content of the service will also be conditioned by the religious level of the people attending. The aim will be to enable them to offer the best of which they are capable.

Where it is necessary for more than one minister to take part in the conduct of the service, it is advisable for the preacher himself

M

to conduct the time of devotion which follows his address. Lesson and Bidding can be allotted to other ministers. Also, it is possible to arrange the introductory versicles and responses for two ministers and the congregation, thus:

1st Minister. Lord, thou hast been our refuge: from one generation to another.

2nd Minister. Before the mountains were brought forth, or ever the heavens and the earth were made:

People. Thou art God from everlasting.

1st Minister. God so loved the world, that he gave his only begotten Son,

2nd Minister. That whosoever believeth in him should not perish:

People. But have everlasting life.

Etc., etc.

VERSICLES AND RESPONSES FROM THE PSALMS

(Though in some cases a plural has been substituted for a singular, in order to be more appropriate for our purpose, and occasionally a section of a verse has been omitted, for the most part these verses are reproduced as they stand in the Psalter.)

1. PRAISE

V. I will give thanks unto the Lord according to his righteousness.

R. And I will praise the Name of the Lord most High.

V. O Lord our Governor.

R. How excellent is thy Name in all the world.

V. The heavens declare the glory of God.

R. And the firmament sheweth his handiwork.

V. The earth is the Lord's.

R. And all they that dwell therein.

V. Give the Lord the honour due unto his Name.

R. Worship the Lord with holy worship.

V. Let all the earth fear the Lord.

R. Stand in awe of him, all ye that dwell in the world.

V. O praise the Lord with me.

R. And let us magnify his Name together.

V. All the world shall worship thee.

R. Sing of thee, and praise thy name.

V. Behold now, praise the Lord.

R. All ye servants of the Lord.

V. Lift up your hands in the sanctuary.

R. And praise the Lord.

V. Praise the Lord, O my soul.

R. And all that is within me, praise his holy Name.

V. O praise our God, ye people.
R. And make the voice of his praise to be heard.

V. Let the people praise thee, O God.
R. Let all the people praise thee.

V. Let us come before his presence with thanksgiving.
R. And shew ourselves glad in him with psalms.

V. O worship the Lord in the beauty of holiness.
R. Worship the Lord with holy worship.

V. O come let us worship, and fall down.
R. And kneel before the Lord our maker.

V. For the Lord is gracious; his mercy is everlasting.
R. And his truth endureth from generation to generation.

V. O Lord, how manifold are thy works.
R. In wisdom hast thou made them all.

V. O that men would therefore praise the Lord.
R. And declare the wonders that He doeth for the children of men.

V. O give thanks unto the Lord, for he is gracious.
R. And his mercy endureth for ever.

V. I will magnify thee, O God, my King.
R. And will praise thy Name for ever and ever.

V. One generation shall praise thy works unto another.
R. And declare Thy power.

2. THANKSGIVING

V. Offer unto God thanksgiving.
R. And let us pay our vows unto the most highest.

V. Unto thee, O God, will we pay our vows.
R. Unto thee will we give thanks.

V. I will thank thee, O Lord my God, with all my heart.
R. And will praise thy Name for ever and ever.

V. Thou art my God, and I will thank thee.

R. Thou art my God, and I will praise thee.

V. O praise the Lord, for it is a good thing to sing praises unto our God.

R. A joyful and pleasant thing it is to be thankful.

V. I will give thanks unto thee, O Lord, with my whole heart.

R. I will speak of all thy marvellous works.

3. PENITENCE

V. O hide not thou thy face from us.

R. Nor cast thy servants away in displeasure.

V. The Lord is nigh unto them that are of a contrite heart.

R. And will save such as be of an humble spirit.

V. Let us take heed to the thing that is right.

R. For that shall bring a man peace at the last.

V. Have mercy upon me, O God, after thy great goodness.

R. According to thy mercy, do away mine offences.

V. For I acknowledge my faults.

R. And my sin is ever before me.

V. Turn thy face from our sins.

R. And blot out all our misdeeds.

V. Make me a clean heart, O God.

R. And renew a right spirit within me.

V. Cast me not away from thy presence.

R. And take not thy holy Spirit from me.

V. The sacrifice of God is a troubled spirit.

R. A contrite heart, O God, shalt thou not despise.

V. Turn us then, O God our Saviour.

R. And let thine anger cease from us.

V. Wilt thou not turn again and quicken us?

R. That thy people may rejoice in thee.

V.   Shew us thy mercy, O Lord.
R.   And grant us thy salvation.

V.   We have sinned with our fathers.
R.   We have done amiss and dealt wickedly.

V.   Keep thy servant from presumptuous sins.
R.   O cleanse me from my secret faults.

V.   Enter not into judgement with thy servants.
R.   For in thy sight shall no man living be justified.

V.   Teach me to do the thing that pleaseth thee.
R.   For thou art my God.

4. FAITH AND TRUST

V.   All the ends of the world shall be turned unto the Lord.
R.   And all the nations shall worship before him.

V.   God is our hope and strength.
R.   Therefore will we not fear.

V.   We wait for thy loving kindness, O God.
R.   For in thee do we trust.

V.   Blessed is the man whose strength is in thee.
R.   In whose heart are thy ways.

V.   Blessed is the people that can rejoice in thee, O Lord.
R.   They shall walk in the light of thy countenance.

V.   Lord, thou hast been our refuge.
R.   From one generation to another.

V.   Before ever the heavens and the earth were made.
R.   Thou art God from everlasting.

V.   Be ye sure that the Lord, he is God.
R.   It is he that hath made us, and not we ourselves.

V.   Lord, thy word endureth for ever.
R.   It giveth light and understanding unto the simple.

V.   Our help standeth in the Name of the Lord.
R.   Who hath made heaven and earth.

V. Except the Lord build the house.

R. Their labour is but lost that build it.

V. Blessed are all they that fear the Lord.

R. And walk in his ways.

V. All nations whom thou hast made shall worship thee, O Lord.

R. And shall glorify thy Name.

V. The fear of the Lord is the beginning of wisdom.

R. Blessed is the man that feareth the Lord.

V. God shall bless his people.

R. And all the ends of the earth shall fear Him.

PRINTED AND BOUND IN GREAT BRITAIN
BY RICHARD CLAY AND COMPANY, LTD.,
BUNGAY, SUFFOLK.